ANALYZING SALES PROMOTION:
Text and Cases

ANALYZING SALES PROMOTION:
Text and Cases

John C. Totten, Ph.D.
Information Resources, Inc.

Martin P. Block, Ph.D.
Northwestern University

Commerce Communications, Inc.
646 W. Wellington
Chicago, IL 60657

Contents

Tables

Figures

Acknowledgements

The authors thank Information Resources, Inc. for providing data from their Marketing Fact Book™ data base. Examples include actual data and analyses of the following products: Pepsi and Coca-Cola; Ragu and Prego spaghetti sauces; Keebler Zesta, Nabisco Premium, and Sunshine Krispy saltines; Huggies, Pampers, and Luv's disposable diapers; Final Touch, Downy, and Snuggle fabric softeners; and Aunt Jemima, Downyflake, and Eggo frozen waffles.

1 *Introduction to Sales Promotion*

One of the first things learned by a beginning student of communications is that the purpose of all communication is to influence behavior. This is why marketers engage in such communications activities as advertising, public relations, product packaging and displays, and sales promotion. The particular behaviors to be influenced may vary widely with the specific marketing situation, and certainly the various tools and techniques may be applied with different levels of effectiveness.

The problem for the marketing manager is to assess the particular marketing situation correctly and then to apply the appropriate tools and techniques. The marketing manager must select the appropriate techniques and develop the most effective executions of those techniques. The manager must understand how the techniques work alone and together to develop the most effective promotional strategy in what is usually an extremely competitive environment.

The best way to develop an understanding of how the techniques work is to examine past experience. This can be done through systematic analysis of past experience to overcome prior beliefs and biases. Such analysis should allow the development of some general principles and guidelines.

The focus of this book is on the analysis of sales promotion effects rather than on the creation of a sales promotion strategy. The purpose is to be able to develop general principles and guidelines to help plan future sales promotion programs. Through the analysis of the cases provided in this book, it is hoped that some discipline is added to the planning and evaluation of sales promotion activity. While this book does not deal specifically with the creative aspects of developing sales promotion programs, it should clearly point to the need for substantially more creativity in the future.

Definition of Sales Promotion

Sales promotion is a collection of many different selling incentives and techniques intended to produce immediate or short-term sales effects. This wide variety makes sales promotion difficult to define in terms of specific activities and techniques. Sales promotion includes coupons, samples, in-pack premiums, self-liquidating premiums, value-packs, refunds and rebates, price-off packs, contests, sweepstakes, trade shows, continuity plans, and

1

others. Perhaps the only unifying theme among these various methods is that they all must be *communicated* to the appropriate audience to be effective. Sales promotion techniques can be applied across a broad range of products, from chewing gum to houses and cars.

The other defining characteristic of sales promotion is that the goal is short-term or *immediate*. Sales promotion is not used to generate long-term results or sales in the future, but rather to generate sales results *now*. The distinction between short-term and long-term may certainly vary with the product category and the particular industry, making a specific time definition somewhat arbitrary. But the important idea is that the goal for sales promotion is results in the current promotional period, and not in subsequent time periods after the promotion ends.

Promotion is then a collection of techniques communicated to target audiences to generate short-term sales results. Traditionally sales promotion has been viewed as a nonrecurrent selling activity, and it is often defined as such. However, this does not reflect the current condition of frequent and repeated sales promotion programs necessary to maintain business in many product categories. In most cases, sales promotion has become an all too recurrent activity, so the idea of a nonrecurrent activity is eliminated from the definition here.

Sales Promotion and Advertising

Sales promotion and advertising are very intimately related. It is difficult to imagine any sales promotion without the support of advertising, and it is becoming increasingly difficult to imagine advertising without the support of sales promotion.

Advertising has been defined many ways, from "salesmanship in print" to "any paid form of non-personal presentation and promotion of ideas, goods, or services by an identified sponsor." The first definition is certainly too broad, since it would also include most public relations activities. The latter definition is better and reflects that advertising is *paid* messages placed in the measured media. The measured media include any medium in one of the four main categories—broadcast, print, traffic, and direct mail—where there is some attempt to estimate the size of the audience for the particular medium. Broadcast media include radio, network television, and cable; print media include magazines and newspapers; traffic media include outdoor and transit; and direct mail includes catalogs and all the other material received in the mail from broadsides to bill stuffers. Omitted from this definition would be specialty advertising, including calendars, key chains, shirts and hats, and similar materials, and a few miscellaneous categories like cinema advertising and directories.

Considerably more is spent each year in sales promotion than in media advertising, with the difference expanding every year as sales promotion spending continues to grow at a faster annual rate. Yet little published material is available on sales promotion.

Advertising can be intended to achieve short-term goals, just like sales promotion, and can also be intended to achieve long-term goals. A major argument for using advertising is its ability to create an enduring brand image in the mind of the consumer. The value of a well-known brand name often can be attributed to a consistent advertising effort over a period of many years.

Advertising can also be used to generate immediate retail sales with newspaper advertisement headlines like "Sale Ends Tomorrow!"

Advertising and sales promotion must work together, since it is advertising that is one of the primary vehicles of communication for sales promotion. The only other major communications vehicles for sales promotion are the product package itself or retail-level in-store displays. Sales promotion would be very limited without its being featured in advertising, although there certainly can be sales promotion activity without any advertising.

A fundamental decision for any marketing manager is the allocation of the budget between advertising and sales promotion. This raises many questions. Should more be spent in sales promotion, and less in advertising, or vice versa? What is the best combination of advertising and sales promotion? Unfortunately these questions do not have simple answers. The only generalization that seems to be almost always true is that advertising and sales promotion work best when they are coordinated and work together.

In recent years the decision between using sales promotion and advertising has been shifting somewhat more in favor of sales promotion. Since 1975, aggregate sales promotion expenditures have grown from just under $30 billion to well over $60 billion in 1983 for an average annual growth rate of 12 percent. As shown in Figure 1-1, this sales promotion growth compares to only a 10 percent annual growth rate for advertising.

Sales Promotion Audiences

Sales promotion efforts can be targeted to three major groups: consumers, the retail trade, and employees. Regardless of the audience, the primary objective for any sales promotion effort is still the same—stimulating short-term sales.

The *consumer* is the ultimate purchaser and user of the product, and sales promotion efforts aimed directly toward this group are normally termed "con-

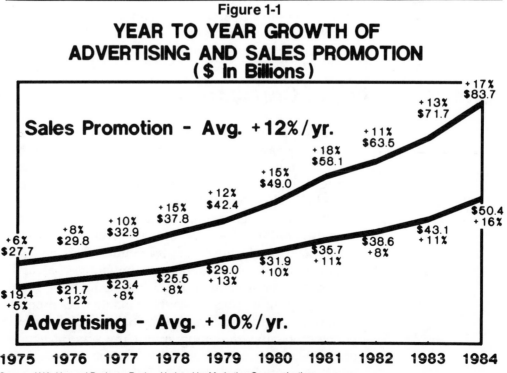

Figure 1-1
YEAR TO YEAR GROWTH OF
ADVERTISING AND SALES PROMOTION
($ In Billions)

Sales Promotion - Avg. +12%/yr.

+17%
$83.7

+13%
$71.7

+11%
$63.5

+18%
$58.1

+15%
$49.0

+12%
$42.4

+15%
$37.8

+10%
$32.9

+8%
$29.8

+6%
$27.7

$50.4
+16%

$43.1
+11%

$38.6
+8%

$35.7
+11%

$31.9
+10%

$29.0
+13%

$25.5
+8%

$23.4
+8%

$21.7
+12%

$19.4
+5%

Advertising - Avg. +10%/yr.

1975 1976 1977 1978 1979 1980 1981 1982 1983 1984

Source: ANA. Harvard Business Review Updated by Marketing Communications

sumer promotions." Defining consumers itself can be a complex problem with several classification schemes commonly used.

Perhaps the most basic way of classifying audiences for consumer sales promotion is distinguishing between "businesses" and "consumers." The common terminology here may be slightly confusing because there are business consumers and non-business consumers, even though both are clearly consumers in the sense of purchasing and using products and services. Consumer promotion is used to refer to both business and consumer when the sales promotion is aimed at the final user of the product. A *consumer* is a private individual purchasing goods and services usually for consumption by self or for consumption by the immediate family. A *business*, normally represented by a purchasing agent, is purchasing goods and services for the operation of business.

The *trade* refers to middlemen and retailers who intend to resell the product or service being promoted to them. *Middlemen* include a wide variety of organizations, including wholesalers, brokers, jobbers, and representatives. *Retailers* are organizations selling directly to consumers as defined above.

The purpose of "trade promotion" is to stimulate the various members of the distribution chain to move the products through, and may have an additional purpose of shifting inventory holding. A trade promotion, then, has the objective of generating resale of the product or service. A particular wholesaler, for example, might receive both consumer and trade promotions. Trade promotions would be intended to stimulate the wholesaler to buy and sell more products. Consumer promotions would be intended to stimulate the wholesaler to buy more products that are consumed in the operation of the business, such as office equipment.

The last group, *employee* promotions, refers to motivational programs usually designed for field sales personnel. Sales contests, both group and individual, are classic examples of the use of sales promotion techniques to motivate employees. An employee suggestion program is another example. Because employee promotions tend to be considered separately, often as part of field sales management, they will not be treated here. The focus here instead will be consumer and trade promotions.

Characteristics of Consumers

Like any marketing strategy, sales promotion needs to be carefully targeted to the appropriate consumer subgroup or market segment. Several ways are used to define consumer groups to target for sales promotion programs.

Segmenting markets is discussed in any introductory marketing textbook. Essentially there are three ways of segmenting consumer markets: demographics and geographics, psychographics, and product usage. *Demographic* segmentation involves defining subgroups according to demographic variables, such as age, income, and gender. This might also include *geographic* segmentation, such as market area or zip code area. This method is particularly useful for selecting advertising media since most media have audience delivery documenting research available in demographic terms. It has also been the most popular and traditional way of describing target markets.

The problem with demographics as a way of segmenting markets for sales promotion is that they generally do not provide sufficiently sensitive discriminations to be able to detect differences between groups. For example, it would be typical to find that the average age and income of women who redeem coupons from a specific promotion are virtually identical to women who do not redeem them. More often than not, demographic differences do not explain any differential effectiveness of a promotional effort. Rather the demographic variables seem to define the limiting parameters of the market itself. For this reason, demographics tend not to be used as a way of describing market segments for sales promotion, even though they are readily provided by the advertising media.

Reasoning might suggest that the more subtle differences within a demographic market segment that account for the impact of sales promotion can be explained by psychological differences. Certainly two married women, each 34 years old, with no children, and household incomes of $35,000 per year, could be substantially different in their reactions to a coupon or a contest. The differences might be explained in psychological differences between the women.

The problem with psychological segmentation, or *psychographics*, is the lack of any available measurement method. There is not any standardized, or even moderately well-accepted, method of determining the psychological differences necessary to derive meaningful segments. For this reason, psychological segmentation must also be rejected, although it might become feasible in the future.

Perhaps the closest relevant variable is "deal proneness." Rather than attempting to understand the underlying psychological process, *deal proneness* simply is a measure of past behavior. The average consumer makes about one-third of the purchases of food store package goods using some form of sales promotion. Those consumers that make a greater than average proportion of their purchases using some form of sales promotion would be placed in a more deal prone classification. Those who make a less than average proportion of purchases using sales promotion would be placed in a less deal prone or a not deal prone classification. The deal prone classification is generally applied with respect to a specific product category, rather than a classification of overall consumer behavior.

Product usage is an increasingly popular method of segmenting markets. The fundamental idea is that some individuals never purchase the product. These individuals are termed "non-users" of the product. Those that do purchase the product, usually with respect to some time span appropriate to product usage, are divided into subcategories according to the volume or frequency of purchase. These subcategories are normally termed *light-user*, *medium-user*, and *heavy-user*, depending on the amount of the product purchased. As will be discussed later, the concept of product usage is quite useful in evaluating sales promotion programs.

Product usage depends upon the purchase cycle of a product. The *purchase cycle* is the average amount of time between purchases. A more frequently purchased product would require a shorter time interval to determine the level of product usage than a less frequently purchased product.

Not only is the purchase of a product important, but also important is the choice of brand within the product category. Generally many brand choices are available, including, in some cases, products with no brands at all, such as "generics." What seems to be important to sales promotion programs is the relative position in the marketplace of a particular brand. A dominant brand, one with more than 40 percent share of the market, may respond differently to sales promotion than a competitive brand, one with approximately 20 percent share of the market. A minor brand, one with less than 5 percent share of the market, may respond differently yet. The difference in the response should be in part attributable to the consumer's perception of the position of the brand. Premium priced products may respond quite differently to sales promotion than a lower priced product.

A related concept is brand loyalty. A user of a product category can be considered *brand loyal* if the same brand is nearly always purchased, and a *brand switcher* if past purchasing history shows no dominant brand. A brand loyal individual would probably respond differently to sales promotion from competing brands than would a brand switcher.

The problem with the concept of brand switching is that it is quite difficult to find individuals who exclusively purchase only one brand over an extended period of time. Normally a brand loyal individual is defined as an individual who usually purchases a single brand allowing for occasional purchases of other brands. A typical definition might be one who makes 80 percent of the purchases of one brand within the product category over a specified time interval. Those who purchase less than this criterion would be defined as brand switchers. Individuals with limited purchase history, such as three or fewer purchases in the period under study might be separated out as *light buyers*, whose loyalty, or lack thereof, cannot be determined.

Deal proneness, product usage, purchase cycle, brand position, and brand loyalty are all important consumer characteristics in evaluating sales promotion programs. Also, while consumers are normally thought of in these terms, the same concepts could apply equally well to businesses. The differences would most likely be found in the characteristics of the product category.

Types of Sales Promotion

There are two ways of categorizing types of sales promotion: their source and their fundamental appeal. Generally there are two sources of sales promotion programs: manufacturers and retailers. Sales promotions that emanate from manufacturers are termed *manufacturer promotions*. Promotions that proceed from a retailer are variously termed *retailer* or *store promotions*.

Retailer promotions may or may not directly result from a manufacturer's trade promotion. In other words, a retailer may offer consumers a promotion because it received a special promotion from a manufacturer. It is, however, the option of the retailer whether or not to offer a promotion to the consumer in response to the manufacturer's trade promotion. A retailer may also offer promotions to consumers without the benefit of a trade promotion, and it is certainly possible that a retailer may not offer any promotion or special price to the consumer even when a trade promotion is provided to that retailer.

There are essentially two primary types of appeals in sales promotion: interest and price. While it can certainly be argued that price is interesting, price is so pervasive as a sales promotion technique that it deserves separate consideration. Examples of price promotions are price-offs, coupons, bonus packs, refund offers, continuity plans, and special pack promotions.

Interest focuses on things other than price. Examples of interest promotions include free premiums, mail-in premiums, samples, contests, and sweepstakes.

Trade promotions might be considered a third category, even though they almost always involve price in the form of a trade allowance. This, however, does not preclude the use of interest promotions to the trade.

Beliefs About Consumer Sales Promotion

Over the years many traditions and beliefs have evolved about how sales promotion works with consumers. Perhaps the most pervasive belief about sales promotion of all types is that it can reinforce advertising and other promotional programs. Sales promotion is normally described as a tool to get more out of advertising campaigns, and it would of course reinforce the same objectives as the advertising.

Apart from advertising, consumer sales promotion as a separate entity is generally thought to be able to accomplish four possible objectives. These objectives seem to be widely accepted and are often used to justify the use of sales promotion.

Obtaining Product Trial

Getting consumers to try a product is fundamental to many marketing strategies. This might involve the introduction of a new product or the attempt to reach new customers who have had no previous experience with the product. In addition, sometimes a long-existing product that has been experiencing a sales decline can be revived by reintroducing it to consumers who may have forgotten about it.

Encouraging Repeat Usage

Once a consumer has tried a product, it is necessary to get the consumer to purchase the product again. An important consideration is that the consumer is generally in a very competitive environment. For that reason often an additional incentive is necessary to keep competitors from winning the consumers back after a successful initial trial. One of the many sales promotion techniques discussed here can be used for this purpose.

Encouraging More Frequent Usage

An important source of business may be in encouraging light and medium users of a product category to become heavy users. Encouraging existing users either to purchase with greater frequency or to purchase in greater quantities can have considerable impact on the size of the market. A related objective is to cause the consumer to trade-up to a more expensive line.

Neutralizing Competition

One of the most common responses a marketing manager might give to justify a sales promotion program is to defuse competitive advertising and sales promotion programs. Sales promotion can be used to hold current customers against competitive promotions by offering similar incentives. Sales promotion is also believed to be able to take consumers out of the market by encouraging them to "load the pantry." Encouraging consumers to buy a large volume of a product presumably makes them immune to competitive advertising and sales promotion pressure. Retailers may use pricing and promotion to signal to competitors. Common programs for this purpose are built around such themes as "We'll match the price of Competitor X," or "We'll redeem the coupons of Competitor X."

Beliefs About Trade Sales Promotion

Like consumer sales promotion, there are persistent beliefs about how sales promotion works with the trade. The most widespread belief is that promoting to the trade is indirectly promoting to the consumer. As a result of the incentive provided from the manufacturer, the trade will provide incentives and programs themselves to the consumer. Trade promotions are commonly thought to be able to accomplish three specific objectives.

Obtaining In-Store Support

Retailers are often in an adversarial position with manufacturers, negotiating over price and supply. Retailers certainly do not automatically cooperate with manufacturer promotional programs and in-store displays, as retailers are literally swamped with material from most competing products. It is commonly believed that it is necessary to provide incentives to the trade to obtain even minimal levels of cooperation to execute any in-store promotional strategies.

Manipulating Trade Inventories

Manipulating trade inventories means getting retailers and wholesalers to either increase or decrease the inventories they carry in their warehouses and stores. Getting wholesalers and retailers to increase their inventories normally requires special incentives. This is because the trade, recognizing that maintaining inventory is a major expense, needs an incentive to offset the cost. If a manufacturer needs to shift inventory to the trade, sales promotion is a powerful tool. Or, the manufacturer may wish to reduce the trade inventory, especially if a product is obsolete, dated, or being replaced by a new line.

Expanding Product Distribution

Perhaps one of the most competitive struggles in marketing is the fight for shelf space. Getting distribution and shelf space is certainly a prerequisite to selling any product, and sales promotion is a means of obtaining it. Hence, introducing a new product requires a substantial promotional effort.

Price Promotional Techniques

There are several ways price can be used as a promotional device, from price-offs to refund offers. The essential difference in the techniques is the way the special price is offered and communicated to the consumer.

Price-Offs

A manufacturer price-off is printed directly on the product packaging and becomes an integral part of the product's appearance to the consumers. Special labels might also be used. A retailer can simply mark down the price on the price label and shelf label.

The advantage of price-offs is that they are easy for the consumer to use, and they place the product in direct competition on the shelf with other brands. Another advantage is that distribution of the promotion, or the price-off, is on the product itself. One disadvantage is that everyone who purchases the product takes advantage of the price reduction, including those who would have purchased the product at the regular price. Another disadvantage is that the shopper may not notice the special price.

Coupons

Overwhelmingly the most common form of sales promotion, coupons account for approximately two-thirds of all sales promotional efforts. Couponing has been growing dramatically in recent years, and now it is common to read about coupon clutter as a major problem just as television commercial clutter has been discussed in advertising.

There are two basic types of coupons: *manufacturer coupons* that have everything paid for by the manufacturer, and *store* or *retailer coupons* that are paid for at least partially by the retailer. Sometimes a cooperative agreement may be in force between the manufacturer and retailer. Normally the distribution of manufacturer coupons is paid for by the manufacturer and the distribution of store coupons is financed by the retailer.

There are numerous variations of coupons.

Cents-Off. The product to be purchased is offered at a certain dollar amount off the regular price.

Free. A free product is given.

Buy One/Get One Free. With the purchase of a product at the regular price, a second is given free.

Time Release. Several cents-off coupons are positioned together with different expiration dates.

Multiple Purchase. This is a coupon offer that applies only when more than one unit of the product is purchased.

Self-Destruct or Option. Two or more coupons are printed over each other in an overlap manner so that both cannot be used and the consumer must choose which to redeem.

Personalized. A coupon that is localized by geographic location or store is redeemable accordingly.

Cross-Ruff. A coupon for one product is obtained with the purchase of another unrelated product.

Related Sale. A coupon received from the purchase of one product is for another product that is related in some way to the purchased product.

Sweepstakes Entry. The redeemed coupon becomes an automatic entry into a sweepstakes.

Coupons can become complex combinations of offers, and are sometimes difficult to classify. A major problem with coupons, as will be discussed later, is getting them distributed to the appropriate consumers.

Coupons offer many advantages in that they create strong pull among consumers, provide quick response, may cost less than other methods such as price-offs (not everyone redeems coupons) or sampling, and may provide support to the sales force in obtaining good trade support that translates into distribution and shelf space.

The disadvantages of coupons are the clutter and the problem of misredemption and mishandling by the trade. Coupon misredemption is a major problem for both manufacturers and retailers. For a new brand, coupons may stimulate additional triers to purchase the brand. For a more established brand, coupons are primarily redeemed by loyal users and by switchers and may generate little incremental business to the brand. Coupon redemptions occur over time, and may cause budgetary problems if levels of redemption and the timing of redemptions are not accurately forecast.

Bonus Packs Another way the consumer can be offered a special price is to increase the amount of the product offered for the same price. The advantages of bonus packs are an increase of the shelf space and distribution and an encouragement to the consumer to buy more of the product. The disadvantages are that it does not enhance the long-term image of the product, or produce loyal users, and it can often be easily pilfered by the trade. As with price-off offers, it may go unnoticed by those consumers not already predisposed to purchase the brand.

Continuity Plans

Another technique requires the saving of some device related to purchase, such as stamps, that can be used for prizes or reduced prices. Some classic examples are savings stamps and the airline frequent flyer plans. The advantages of continuity plans are the requirement for high purchase frequency, the relative ease of implementation, and the extension of the purchase habit. The disadvantages are limited appeal, little trade support, and little or no in-store display. Grocery retailers frequently use continuity plans to stimulate repeated visits to the store. A typical plan might offer one volume of an encyclopedia or one item in a cookware set each week.

Refunds

When the purchaser sends in a proof of purchase, a refund or rebate is provided. The major advantage is that not everyone who purchases the product requests the refund. Other advantages are that they are relatively inexpensive, that the sales force likes them, and that the trade likes them because refund offers are generally easy to display. The disadvantages are that the results are difficult to measure, and that refund offers typically do not generate trial, and may be used primarily by already brand-loyal consumers.

Trade Promotions

Trade promotions generally take one of two forms: the trade allowance or the trade coupon. Both are clearly forms of price promotion, but the special price is offered to the trade rather than directly to the consumer. A *trade allowance* is a price discount that can take a variety of forms depending upon the product category. Sometimes a trade allowance might be based upon case lots; sometimes it might be based upon a dollar sales volume, or upon other measures of sales. A *trade coupon*, like coupons to consumers, offers the trade a special price offer when redeemed with purchase from the manufacturer.

Interest Promotion Techniques

Some promotion techniques attempt to stimulate interest, other than price, in order to generate short-term sales. Often the particular interest might be in products, activities, or special events. A common promotional technique is to create special events, such as contests or sweepstakes. There are several techniques that fit this general category.

Sampling

Providing the consumer with a free sample of the product is a very effective means of introducing a new product or demonstrating an improvement in an existing product. Typically a small "trial" size is provided, and as with coupons, the major problem is distribution of the product samples. Sometimes they can be delivered through the mass media, such as newspapers. Sometimes they must be delivered door-to-door, or distributed by salesmen, or perhaps even mailed.

The advantages of sampling are that it initiates trial, and may indirectly force distribution and in-store display because it may create store traffic. The disadvantages of sampling are that it is generally very expensive, may be difficult to distribute to the precise target audience, and wasteful if the sample is discarded without trial.

Contests and Sweepstakes

The difference between contests and sweepstakes is primarily that contests require purchase of the product to become eligible to win, while sweepstakes do not. If a purchase is required, the sweepstakes may be interpreted as a lottery and may be illegal in some states. By definition, contests require skill to win, whereas sweepstakes require only a simple "ballot" entry that is drawn at random to win.

Contests and sweepstakes are used to create interest in advertising, to gain shelf space, to increase trial or product image, or to increase store traffic. The advantages of contests and sweepstakes are building store traffic, ease of controlling associated costs, and generating media publicity. The disadvantages are the proliferation and clutter associated with contests and the "professional" participators who collect and enter all available contests and sweepstakes but are not potential customers for the product.

Free Premiums

There are several types of free premiums, including in- or on-pack premiums, such as a toy or gift, or a reusable container, and eligibility to purchase other products at a lower cost. Free premiums presumably extend the image of the product and increase the product's perceived value.

The advantages of free premiums are gaining display and differentiating the product. The disadvantages are the reduction of sales if the premium is not desirable, trade resistance if the premium is being sold elsewhere in the store, and possible pilfering and abuse in channels of distribution.

Mail-In Premiums

There are several types of mail-in premiums, including self-liquidating premiums, free-in-the-mail premiums, and speed plans. *Self-liquidating premiums* are sold with proofs of purchase at just over wholesale cost of the premium item. The premium does not cost the promoter anything because it is resold at the purchase cost. *Free-in-the-mail premiums* are free gifts that are sent with proof of purchase. The cost is entirely borne by the promoter. *Speed plans* offer the consumer different prices or prizes depending upon the number of proofs of purchase that are accumulated.

Mail-in premiums can be used to reinforce a product image or the product's advertising, increase advertising attention, generate trial, reward multiple purchases, and gain trade support. The advantages of mail-in premiums are that they often require multiple purchases and that they attract attention. The disadvantages are that trial may not necessarily be obtained, it is difficult to measure the impact on sales, and usually, few consumers tend to take advantage of mail-in premium offers.

Legal Considerations

Sales promotion is controlled by three general areas of regulation: federal antitrust law, the Federal Trade Commission (FTC) and Food and Drug Administration (FDA), and state law. Federal antitrust law begins with the Sherman Act and includes the later Robinson-Patman Act and Clayton Act. Essentially the antritrust law forbids practices that hinder competition and that favor one competitor over others. Usually small retailers may have difficulty competing with the large retail chains.

Antitrust law affects sales promotion by regulating trade allowances and related practices. A trade allowance must be non-discriminatory so that large retailers are not favored over small ones. A small retailer must be able to participate as well as the large retailer.

The FTC is clearly an extension of antitrust law and requires that the manufacturer notify all retailers about a promotional program. The FTC also requires that the manufacturer not pay the retailer unless the retailer performs as required: that is, use the in-store display material or whatever.

The FTC and FDA both have guidelines regarding the use of cents-off labels. A cents-off label can only be used if the product has been sold at the normal price in the trading area during the preceding 30 days and the savings to the consumer and the retailer is at least as much as the savings represented. Also the cents-off sales volume may represent not more than 50 percent of the total sales volume of the product in a 12-month period. The retailer is obligated to display the regular price along with the cents-off price. The FDA requires information on expiration dates and offer conditions to be on the label, as well.

State laws generally apply to lotteries and govern contests and sweepstakes. If a prize is to be awarded, then both consideration and chance become legal elements. Consideration refers to the expenditure of money or substantial effort required in order to enter. Chance is not present if through the exercise of sufficient intelligence and diligence the entrant can win the prize. If lots are drawn, then obviously chance is present. In the former situation, the promotion is a contest, and legal in most states; the latter situation is a lottery or a sweepstakes depending upon the consideration involved. Lotteries are generally not legal in most states, while sweepstakes, with little or no consideration, generally are legal. Legal concerns in sales promotion are complex and involve several layers of government. Legal counsel should be consulted when planning a promotional program.

Point-of-Purchase Displays

Displaying the product inside the store is a major component of any selling strategy. Any additional material in the store beyond the product itself is generally referred to as point-of-purchase advertising. All signs, displays, devices, and structures used as sales aids can be included in the definition. The material can be as simple as a printed card, or as complicated as elaborate illuminated and animated structures that draw attention to special displays of the product. Included in point-of-purchase advertising would be window signs and displays, banners, counter and check-out displays, interior and exterior wall signs, merchandise racks, trays and cases for both counters and aisles, shelf edgers, and can toppers. Point-of-purchase includes a wide variety of material.

Point-of-purchase advertising material can be provided by the manufacturer or by the retailer. It is probably a reasonable generalization to say that most manufacturer-provided point-of-purchase material would appear to be more expensively produced and perhaps more elaborate. Retailer-provided material would tend to appear to be more "homemade" and probably less elaborate. In general the retailer would be interested in short-term results, whereas the manufacturer would be interested in somewhat longer term results.

Whether the material is provided by either the manufacturer or retailer, the point-of-purchase material can take advantage of virtually any of the sales promotion techniques described before. Retailer provided material is probably more likely to use one of the price promotion techniques than is manufacturer provided material.

Advertising Support

It is important that any sales promotion program be supported with some paid media advertising. While sales promotion programs are supported in all media, probably the print media are the most important because they lend themselves to the delivery of coupons.

Print advertising media are the major method of distribution of coupons, with less than 20 percent delivered by other means, including both in- and on-pack coupons and instant coupons, those provided at the check-out counter or at the product location in the store.

Newspapers have the overwhelming share of the coupon distribution volume, but they deliver coupons in several ways. The largest proportion is through free standing inserts, which account for well over half of the coupons distributed. Free standing inserts offer the advantage of high quality color reproduction and have been growing very rapidly in recent years. The next largest newspaper category is ROP, or run-of-paper, display advertising. Also included for newspapers would be Sunday supplements and comics, but these represent a very small proportion. Magazines and direct mail deliver approximately 10 percent of the coupons.

Beyond delivery of coupons, advertising is certainly the most common source of the sales promotion message. Contests and sweepstakes, premium offers, and other price promotions are commonly included in advertising. Both the manufacturer and the retailer make heavy use of promotion in their advertising. The manufacturer would be somewhat more likely to use interest promotion techniques, and the retailer somewhat more likely to use price promotion techniques. However, it should be remembered that coupons are the most common form of sales promotion and widely used by both manufacturers and retailers.

Cooperative advertising also plays an important role in supporting sales promotion programs. *Cooperative advertising* is a form of advertising where the cost is shared by both the manufacturer and the retailer. Generally the copy, in ready to run form, is provided by the manufacturer. The retailer needs only to add the local address to the copy, which is easily done by the local newspaper, radio, or television station. The retailer buys the space or time, taking advantage of local advertising rates. The manufacturer pays some proportion of the time or space.

Cooperative advertising, or co-op, agreements are tremendously varied between the manufacturer and retailer. Variation in the particular requirements of a manufacturer and the proportion of payment make co-op a sufficiently complex subject to fill a book by itself. Cooperative advertising becomes a form of trade promotion itself, just like a trade allowance.

Even when a local retailer runs price-offs and coupons in weekly newspaper advertising, the advertising is clearly being used to support the promotion. In fact the importance of the advertising support can be seen with the number of in-store "unadvertised" price specials that many retailers use.

Any time that a promotion is included in the advertising, the promotion will be termed as being *featured* in this book. Any time that a promotion is included in any point-of-purchase displays in the store, the promotion will be termed as being *displayed* in this book. In many marketing areas, newspapers will have a special section once a week devoted to food and food-related items. These "Best Food Day" issues will have a disproportionate amount of ROP manufacturer coupons, and are the primary choice for grocery retailers in placing ad features and store coupons. Drug store and mass merchandiser print advertisements tend to be more concentrated in weekend editions.

Sales Promotion in Action

"Best Food Day" ads run the gamut of formats. Figure 1-2 (upper right) shows a full-page ROP ad with large pictures of relatively few items. Figure 1-3 (above) is also a full-page ROP ad with medium-sized pictures of most featured items. Figure 1-4 (left) is a full-page ROP high-density ad with many products listed, but relatively few pictures.

Fancy Feast (above) offers multiple purchase coupon. Sprite (right) uses a self-destruct option coupon. Zesta (left) uses a cross-ruff on-pack coupon with Snickers candy bars.

Blue Bonnet margarine offers a coupon good for a free product (above left). Burger King gives multiple coupons, including "Buy one/Get one free", plus different time expiration dates (bottom left). Carol Wright announces a sweepstakes to go along with its mail-order offers (above). Taster's Choice coffee adds coupon to its premium offer of a free coffee cup (below).

Baby Ruth candy bars use POP display to offer free "Goonies" poster (above). The candy was a key feature in the "Goonies" movie. Many supermarkets use continuity programs to retain customers. One example is Dominick's in Chicago, with its offer of porcelain cookware (left). Many products use refund offers. An example is Comtrex (below).

2 *Analysis Techniques*

To really understand how sales promotion works, it is necessary to go beyond description of the techniques and observe them in operation. Sales promotion programs need to be applied to real marketing problems with the results carefully analyzed. This needs to be done over an extended period of time to be able to generalize and begin to develop some principles of sales promotion that will be usable by the marketing manager.

Until recently sales promotion has been managed primarily on the basis of traditional and anecdotal understanding of how it works. Neither the necessary data nor the computing power has been available to do any systematic analysis. This has now completely changed, forcing complete analysis of any sales promotion effort along with careful management in order to remain competitive in the future.

Assessing the Impact of Sales Promotion

The computer revolution that has swept the business world is just now beginning to alter the traditional methods of establishing product prices, assessing the impact of price changes, and assessing the impact of promotional activity. Computer technology has made possible the collection of purchase and sales data in ways that were previously not possible, and has greatly enhanced the ability to manipulate and to analyze that data.

There are two factors that emerge as driving forces in the move toward analysis of sales promotion. They are improved cost accounting and availability of information on sales performance down to the level of individual items at individual retail outlets.

Improved Cost Accounting Improved accuracy of cost accounting methods by both the manufacturer and the retailer is providing the capability to allocate more accurately both fixed and variable costs on a brand by brand, size of package by size of package basis. It is quite common for manufacturers to carry a line of differentiated products within a single category, with several package sizes for each product. Each manufacturer can easily have dozens of different products in the same product category. Obviously, the addition of a differentiated product, such as a different flavor or a different package size, greatly aggravates the accounting problem as there are simply more items. However, the addition of each brand, extension, or size is justified on the basis of expanded sales volume, as the additions usually provide additional consumer benefits of more product choice and greater convenience of product use.

The proliferation of items has led to difficulty in determining if all items are justified on the basis of their contribution to profit. However, with the ever-decreasing cost of collecting and processing data by computers, historical data on cost can be kept on the finest level of detail.

The retailer cost accounting problem might even appear to be worse than that faced by the manufacturer. A typical retail outlet in grocery, drug, or mass merchandising may handle from 15,000 to 30,000 individual items in 300 to 400 different product categories. Movement from the store of many individual items may be quite small, hardly justifying individual by-hand analysis, except on an infrequent basis in making retain or drop decisions on shelf stocking. In response to the problem retailers have adopted simple pricing formulas such as:

$$\text{Selling Price} = \text{Purchase Price} + 20\%$$

The simple percent mark-up rule is a typical method of management for many retailers. The percentage is adjusted to cover overall fixed costs, variable costs, and profit.

Mark-ups may vary across product classes based on easily identified differential operating costs. A grocery meat department, for example, may require special processing and storage equipment, and have a relatively high product loss rate due to the relatively short shelf life. Refrigerated items may require special storage and display equipment. Many produce and dairy items also have limited shelf lives. Considerations like these may dictate differential mark-ups on a department-by-department basis.

The use of computerized techniques has made more accurate accounting possible and has greatly improved cost allocation making the department-by-department approach feasible. The largest gains in allocating costs appear to be generated through analysis of operations required from the initial order of the product through the final sale to a consumer. Today there are systems which can estimate costs on an item-by-item basis. These systems are generally called DPP (Direct Product Profitability) systems and are available from several sources.

Improved Data

Before the computer was employed at the grocery check-out lane, there was virtually no individual purchase data available. The growth of automated check-out devices, or scanners, has been justified by most retailers on the basis of improved check-out productivity; that is, reduced labor and reduced error in entering prices. The management value of the data has been generally ignored.

A by-product of such automatic check-out device installation is an accurate recording on an outlet-by-outlet basis of the prices charged and the sales volume for each item sold on time periods as short as one week. A number of syndicated data services are currently using scanner-collected data to provide client manufacturers a detailed reporting of brand sales volume, competitive pricing, and promotional activity.

Most importantly, the accumulation of detailed historical information on an outlet-by-outlet basis provides a foundation for the statistical analysis of interactions among the pricing and promotional activities of competing brands.

Also critically important is the ability to conduct experiments at the retail outlet level to assess the probable impact of pricing and promotional activities outside the observed range of historical conditions. Previously, such information could be obtained only by manipulating pricing and promotional activity on a much broader scale, such as sales territory level.

The company pioneering this technique, Information Resources Incorporated (IRI), has the most consistent historical data base anywhere to examine the impact of pricing and promotion decisions in grocery product categories. It is this data that is the basis for the cases provided in later chapters and for the concluding sales promotion principles. The IRI data are collected using scanners in grocery stores in several selected markets around the country. The data have been collected for several years. They represent one of the most complete data bases on grocery product sales available anywhere. The particular methodology will be discussed in more detail later.

Limitations   There are two important limitations to the application of scanner data to sales promotion problems. The first limitation is that no psychological variables are measured or recorded. The effects measured record the overt behavior of product purchase. Some questions, such as the long-term impact of sales promotion programs on the image of the brand, cannot be directly addressed. It can certainly be argued, however, that such questions are not particularly important given that sales are so well measured.

At the time of this writing, historical data on some product categories are not available. Few durable goods, for example, are recorded in commercially available data bases. To date, data suppliers have concentrated on product categories sold through grocery stores, supermarkets, and drug stores. Hence, the generalizations drawn here are based upon frequently purchased non-durable package goods product categories only. The analysis methods described, however, apply generally to scanner-collected sales data.

Sales Promotion Decisions

Before the new data and analytic techniques can be brought to bear on any specific sales promotion problem, it is necessary to establish objectives for that promotion. In order to evaluate any promotional effort, it is first necessary to understand the goals for that promotion.

Setting Objectives   The first step is always setting objectives. Objectives for sales promotion, like objectives for any marketing strategy, must be unambiguous and realistic. The objectives need to be unambiguous in that they must provide for *measurable* outcomes. Providing an "incentive to consumers," for example, is not adequate because it does not provide for a measurable outcome whereby a manager could determine whether or not the promotion was a success. The objective of "increasing sales by 100,000 units," however, is quite precise and measurable, assuming that the appropriate system is in place. Objectives may be stated in terms of volume sales, share of market, profitability, trial of product among previous non-users, or changes in inventory position.

It is also important that objectives be realistic in terms of their potential to be fulfilled. Objectives that could never be reached should be avoided since they make the entire process unworkable and as difficult to manage as though there were no objectives at all.

Price and Promotion

In most analyses of sales promotion activity, it is best to separate the decision about the pricing of the product from any decision about using sales promotion. A product should have an established normal selling price that consumers expect to pay. This price is certainly influenced both by the costs incurred by the manufacturer and by the retailer, but it is not necessarily entirely determined by them.

Rational manufacturers certainly would not as normal practice sell any established product below its variable cost of production. Retailers sometimes sell limited numbers of items below cost when it is believed that such items are influential in attracting new shoppers to the store, building overall sales volume. In cases where a product would be sold below cost, it would usually be wise to avoid incurring additional costs such as storage costs.

There are two basic ways of determining the selling price of a particular product. The first and simplest way is to apply a simple mark-up rule, such as 20 percent of cost. In other words, if a mythical product costs 80¢ from the manufacturer, the retailer can then apply the mark-up rule, in this case 20 percent, and add 20 percent of 80¢ or 16¢. The selling price to the consumer is the 80¢ plus 16¢, or 96¢. This price would probably be psychologically adjusted to 99¢.

The cost-plus pricing approach, simply applying the mark-up rule, has a major disadvantage in that it relies on historical costs, and ignores the operation of the marketplace. This can mean substantial lost profits. Often a retailer may sell a product at too low a price using this method. A much better method is that borrowed from microeconomics, which uses a simple demand curve.

A *demand curve* is the relationship between the selling price of the product and the number of units of that product that are sold. In general, lower prices would mean higher unit sales and higher prices would mean lower unit sales. While there are sometimes exceptions, such as special products like perfume sold on the basis of style or prestige, lower prices usually lead to increased unit sales.

The biggest problem for both the manufacturer and retailer is being able to estimate enough of the demand curve to be able to determine the estimated sales levels at alternative selling prices. Traditional methods, such as quarterly or annual sales levels, simply do not provide sufficient data. That leaves subjective methods, like best-guess estimates from appropriate personnel, or very expensive experimentation. Scanner-based sales reporting can provide sufficient data to do relatively inexpensive experimentation.

Because scanning records every purchase of a product instantly, comparisons can be made on virtually a day-to-day store-by-store basis. Products can be analyzed on a very short time interval, such as a day or a week, or over a very long time, such as months or years. Comparison of natural or promotion-induced price changes with sales volume can then provide a most reasonable estimate of the fundamental demand curve for that product. Relatively few stores are required for experimenting with new price levels. Almost always, determining the nature of the demand curve for the product will be the first step in analyzing any sales promotion. (See Figure 2-1.)

Those with previous exposure to economics will note that in this text we use the microeconomic convention that in the short run quantity sold is determined by price. We thus place price on the horizontal axis and quantity on the vertical axis. The macroeconomic convention of using price on the vertical axis

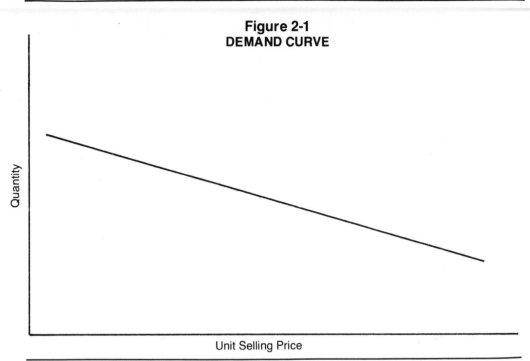

Figure 2-1
DEMAND CURVE

and quantity on the horizontal axis stems from the assumption that over long periods of time, price levels are determined by the quantity demanded.

Once the demand curve has been determined, then costs can be directly compared. Costs usually are divided into major components: fixed costs and variable costs. *Fixed costs* do not change with sales volume and are incurred even if none of the product is sold. *Variable costs* change with the sale of the product and are normally directly related to the volume of the product sold. For example, gasoline requires a storage tank and pump to be sold at retail. The net expense of the pump and related equipment would be fixed cost. The electrical power needed to operate the pump and the maintenance expense would be directly related to the volume of gasoline sold and would be variable costs, as would be the cost of purchasing gasoline from the refiner or area distributor.

By converting the unit selling price to revenue and cost, a break-even chart can be prepared. Revenue results from multiplying the appropriate quantity and the selling price. Total cost results from multiplying the fixed and variable unit cost and the appropriate quanitity. Total revenue and total cost curves can then be plotted against the quantity sold. When the total revenue curve is above the total cost curve, then profit is earned. When the total cost curve is above the total revenue curve, then there is a loss. The point where the total revenue curve and the total cost curve intersect is the break-even point. (See Figure 2-2.)

From a marketing management perspective, the important variables are the price and the profit, not the quantity. A third graph or chart combines the demand curve and break-even chart and compares the unit selling price with revenue and cost. A price-profit chart, as shown in Figure 2-3, is a convenient way to assess the impact of various price levels on ultimate profit levels.

How these charts are used depends to some extent on the managerial policy of the particular organization. For example, profit can be viewed in terms of

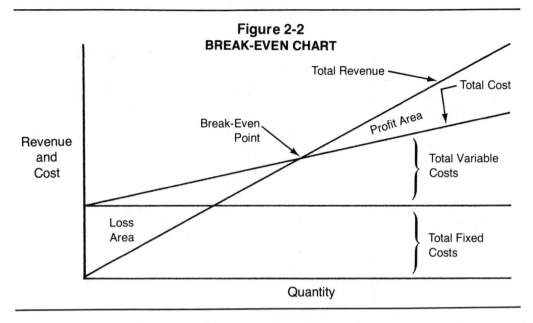

Figure 2-2
BREAK-EVEN CHART

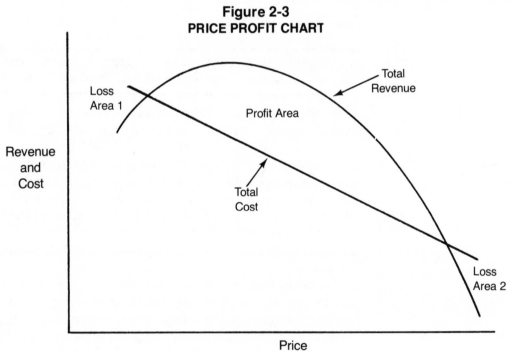

Figure 2-3
PRICE PROFIT CHART

Loss area 1, with price too low to cover costs, always exists.
Loss area 2, where high prices drive quantity so low that costs are not covered, may be nearly non-existent (e.g. luxury items), or may be critical (e.g. commodity items).

absolute dollars or amount, or it can be viewed in terms of a percentage or rate. It often happens that one price level would result in the highest rate of profit, and another price level would result in the greatest amount of profit. The choice, of course, would depend upon how the management of the organization views profit and rate of return.

These charts provide a convenient framework for analyzing price and promotion decisions. By holding some of the variables constant, such as the normal selling price and the cost of goods sold, then the impact of promotion can easily be examined. The difficult problem is to be able to understand the impact on the sales volume; the solution normally requires research.

Evaluation and Research

Establishing the relationship between selling price and unit sales requires careful study of product sales at the retail level. It is critically important that sales be studied at the retail level, the level where the product is ultimately sold.

For the manufacturer, examining sales at the manufacturer level can be very misleading as the product can languish in wholesaler and retailer inventories for long periods of time before being sold to a consumer. Manufacturer shipments reflect the aggregate effects of the way particular manufacturer deal offerings are translated by the retail trade. The manufacturer can assess with reasonable accuracy the incremental volume and profit generated by the offer, but seldom gains insight into the way in which alternative terms might influence volume and profit. However, if retailers purchase extra volume at the promotion price, for later resale at normal retail price (forward buying) then estimates of incremental volume may be biased. Information on competitive manufacturers' pricing and promotional activity is difficult to incorporate in an analysis of shipments. Marketers must do substantially more than merely examine their own sales records.

Obtaining an accurate measure of retail sales is necessary to properly evaluate the effectiveness of sales promotion programs, and requires a special research effort to obtain. There are several ways that sales for most product categories can be measured at the retail level, although in certain situations some of the methods may be too expensive to be practical. Probably automobiles are one of the easiest to measure because of the vehicle registration requirements of state governments which provide a natural data base describing the vehicle purchased, the purchase date, and new owner identification. Few product categories, however, have this luxury. The research required is often best performed by external specialized research organizations.

Using Research Service Organizations

For most marketers, contracting for research services with an external research company is common practice. Generally most marketers do not possess the specialized personnel to collect the necessary data. Research service companies are also often in a better position than marketers to contract with retailers and wholesalers for data. It is difficult for a marketer, who is generally in a continuous bargaining position with the trade, to get much information from them on the passthrough of price discounts and the degree of competitive activity.

There are two ways that a marketer can contract with a research service organization: on a custom basis, or on a syndicated basis. *Custom research* means that the information is collected and analyzed for only one client. *Syndicated research* means that the same information is collected and analyzed for more than one client. Each has advantages and disadvantages.

Custom research is known only to the client and the research service organization and is therefore secret or proprietary. It also has the advantage of being flexible in terms of scheduling and method. The primary disadvantage of custom research is that it is expensive, since only one client must pay the entire bill.

Syndicated research, on the other hand, has the advantage of credibility when measures of competitive activity are being taken. If more than one competitor is paying for the research, then there is less reason to suspect any particular bias. Syndicated research is also less expensive, because the cost can be shared among more than one client. The primary disadvantage of syndicated research is a lack of flexibility; it usually requires a fixed schedule and a standardized methodology.

A good application of custom research would be a new product test that a marketer would not want competitors to know about. A good application of syndicated research is the measurement of advertising media audiences or brand market share over time.

An emerging trend is for research companies to collect and summarize sales on a syndicated basis, but further to conduct custom studies on the data base built by the syndicated data collection.

Measuring Product Sales

There are several ways that retail product sales can be measured. Various methods have evolved over the years for different product categories. The methods that have evolved and are described here are all commercial successes. They are all offered for sale by at least one commercial research service organization and, of course, are purchased by marketers.

Store Shelf Audits Most grocery and package goods items are sold today through supermarkets and can be relatively easily monitored. By keeping counts of the movements of products on and off the shelves, an estimate of product sales can be determined for that store. Periodically counting the store's inventory and subtracting the beginning inventory from the ending inventory provides an estimate of the sales for a given period.

The A. C. Nielsen Company has provided a service based upon this method for many years. Using a carefully selected sample of supermarkets throughout the country, Nielsen is able to provide a national estimate of retail market share for most products sold through supermarkets. Nielsen also audits drug stores and other retail outlets. Product sales can be easily estimated by brand and package size. In addition, Nielsen provides estimates of average retail prices, wholesale prices, average store inventory, promotional activity, and advertising. Special merchandising activity, such as premiums or bonus packs, may be noted as well. Nielsen audits the stores every two months.

Audit information such as this is available over extended periods of time, providing an indication of longer run changes in brand or market position. It is generally available on a regional basis as well as nationally, allowing assessment of brand strengths and weaknesses by region.

There are three problems in using shelf audit data to evaluate sales promotion programs. The first and perhaps most obvious problem is that only products sold primarily through supermarkets and drug stores can be studied. If a product has a large proportion of its sales through other outlets, examining only the supermarket portion of the sales could be misleading. Products not sold at all through supermarkets, of course, could not be easily studied.

A second problem is the lack of any information about the consumer. This makes it difficult to study promotional influences aimed at the individual consumer or to consider any targeted impacts on different market segments. Analysis is limited to an aggregate analysis of the entire market.

The third problem is the relatively long time period between measurements. Most promotions are designed to promote immediate response, sometimes within a single day or week. If the measurements are not taken at a frequency at least equal to the expected duration of the impact of the sales promotion program, then too many other factors can impinge on the sales of the product and dilute the effect of the specific promotion. In 1985, Nielsen introduced a scanner based data sales monitoring service to augment store audit information.

Warehouse Withdrawals

Moving back a step in the distribution chain can simplify the monitoring process. Assuming that supermarkets obtain all their inventory from a few central warehouses and knowing that supermarkets tend to avoid maintaining large in-store inventories, much the same information could be obtained by inventorying the warehouses instead of the supermarkets themselves.

Sales Area Marketing Incorporated (SAMI) uses a computerized method of warehouse withdrawal to provide a measurement of sales and distribution of products sold through supermarkets. SAMI provides data nationally and in approximately 50 individual markets.

The warehouse withdrawal method has the same disadvantages as the shelf audit method but lacks the store level information. In addition, there are several important classes of products that are generally delivered directly to the store without intermediate warehousing. These include high-turnover items justifying shipment directly from the manufacturer in truckload lots, and locally produced items, often with limited shelf lives, such as bakery, dairy, or soft drink products.

Mail Consumer Panels

The traditional method of collecting individual consumer level information has been the mail consumer panel. The subjects are recruited through the mail, and respond through the mail with either a purchase diary or questionnaire. The subjects periodically report their purchase behavior, hence the panel design. Some of the research organizations that provide this service also offer telephone service as well.

There are two types of mail panel data collection instruments: the purchase diary and the questionnaire. The *purchase diary* is provided to the subject before the purchases are made and is intended to be completed coincidentally with the purchase. The *questionnaire* method relies on the recall ability of the subject, asking the purchase behavior to be reconstructed from memory for a specified period of time, such as a week or month. The recall questionnaire method is currently the more popular method.

Several research organizations maintain pre-recruited mail panels that can easily be used to measure purchase behavior. They include National Family Opinion (NFO) and Market Facts, Inc. Marketing and Research Counselors, Inc. (M/A/R/C), offers a neighborhood panel in 25 markets that can be invited to central locations for personal interviews if necessary. Most of the mail panel research has been custom research. Mail panels have also been a very popular means of testing new products before any store placement.

Mail panels are often questioned on the representativeness of their samples and on the quality of the data obtained. Not everyone recruited agrees to participate in mail panel research, with some estimates claiming as low as 10 percent of the initial sample agreeing to participate. The mail panel research organizations attempt to counter this problem with very careful balancing of their panels according to geographic areas and demographic characteristics.

Any time that people are asked questions, there is the possibility of error. When recall is used, it is possible that the memory may not be entirely accurate. Comparisons of recall of product purchase versus scanner measured purchase indicate time compression effects. The question, "What products have you used in the last three months?" may yield responses more closely reflecting product usage in the last year. Usage of private label and generic products may be under-reported. It is also possible that the recording of the responses may not be complete, legible, or accurate. Therefore, the quality of the data received through a mail panel is often a problem and requires careful editing and coding.

Mail panels have an advantage because they are able to collect data for virtually any product category. The product need not necessarily be sold through supermarkets or any other particular type of retail outlet. In addition, mail panels are probably still the best way to study durable goods, such as tires and major appliances.

Store Scanner Data

Perhaps the greatest technological innovation in the supermarket in recent years has been the automated checkout lane. Using the universal product bar code, a computer controlled bar code reader identifies the product; the appropriate price is found in a computer maintained data base; and the customer is provided a printout receipt. Each purchase is entered into a data base for later analysis. An average supermarket may record approximately 150,000 such individual purchases in a day. Usually, purchases are summarized to total sales by item on a daily or weekly basis rather than storing all individual transactions.

It is interesting that the supermarkets that have adopted automated checkout systems have not done so because of the value of the data they collect. Instead, the rationale for the adoption usually includes the reduction of clerk checkout error and increased checkout speed.

Automated checkout systems have also made possible the "instant coupon," which is presented to the customer at checkout time for their next purchase. Instant coupons are awarded depending upon products purchased during the current trip. Customers could be given coupons for competing products or the same product to help reinforce repurchase.

The automated checkout data provide all of the characteristics of the package and brand, plus the exact price paid and the purchase quantity. This is considerably more data than are available from the shelf audit method. The data are precisely timed, so that the date and even time of day is known.

There are two problems with scanner data alone. The first is the same as with shelf audit data, they provide no information about the consumer making the purchase. Analyses of different consumer typologies still cannot be done. The other major problem with scanner data is that in most markets not all of the retail outlets are scanned. A consumer may purchase products in a store that is scanned, but then go on to another store that is not. As a result, incomplete coverage of a market might produce very biased understanding of the market if the focus is on consumer behavior.

Several research organizations either have started projects or have announced projects based upon scanner data. One of the research organizations is IRI, which has been using scanner data for several years. Nielsen has been conducting experiments and has announced a scanner-based service. A joint Arbitron and Burke experimental project has also been recently announced. There is little doubt that scanner data are revolutionizing market research.

Store Scanner Panels

The solution to the consumer problem with store scanner data is the store scanner panel. By providing individuals with special cards that can be read by the bar code reader in the store, one can have a complete recording of all scannable purchases by a selected subset of individuals. This combines the advantages of both the store scanner data and the mail consumer panel.

Again, the problem is coverage within the geographical market area. For the system to record all of the purchases of a household, it would be necessary to have all of the retail outlets in the area scanning and participating. IRI has minimized the problem by nearly complete coverage of isolated markets where there are few opportunities for consumers to shop in non-covered outlets. Designed with market research experimentation in mind, the IRI solution allows the manipulation of media, store prices, and store displays.

To provide more national data representativeness, IRI has expanded into syndicated data reporting from major metropolitan markets, although with reduced coverage of household purchasing. Arbitron and Burke are planning to solve the problem by providing each household with an in-home bar code reader to identify products purchased. This solution, however, would still jeopardize store-specific information such as price, promotional activity in stores, and competitive conditions.

The scanner panel has been proven to be a viable alternative and it is the heart of rapidly expanding research services by IRI, Nielsen, and Burke. There is little doubt that other research organizations will follow, making the scanner panel as common a research technique as the telephone interview in the future.

Individual Versus Aggregate Measurement

A major requirement for data used to evaluate sales promotion programs is that they be sufficiently sensitive to detect any differences in response due to promotional activity. Data that are averaged across time may not be sufficiently sensitive because the averaging process may also be averaging away differences due to promotion.

One of the greatest difficulties is that sales promotion is always presented to consumers in a very competitive environment. Promotions are offered to consumers so frequently that the effects of one program are almost immediately countered by another. In addition, the marketplace is extremely dynamic and subject to an extraordinary number of influences.

In many studies of sales promotion programs, it has been found that only data collected at a time period sufficiently small that pricing and promotional activity is constant are sufficiently precise to detect differences attributable to any one promotional effort. When the data are aggregated, the differences tend to disappear. Aggregate data, that is, data summarized beyond the level of the individual retail outlet level on a weekly basis, generally cannot be used to evaluate sales promotion.

Hence, in order to evaluate sales promotion programs effectively, the data must be collected on an individual store week basis, and not aggregated across time, stores, or markets. This point is clearly illustrated in the cases provided in this book in later chapters.

Time Period

Data can be aggregated (summarized) over time. The results need to be measured on a basis consistent with the duration of the promotional event. For a weekend special store sale, daily measurement may be required. For the typical week-long event in many grocery, drug, and mass merchandisers, weekly sales are usually sufficient. Consumer coupons, sweepstakes, and similar promotional events may take several months to achieve full impact.

If data are collected on a less frequent basis, then the impact of an individual promotion may be entirely lost in all the competing promotions that occur later in the week, or even later in the month.

The same problem of aggregation exists with data summarized over several sales outlets with differing promotional conditions. Data analysis techniques exist that attempt to estimate promotional effects from data which have been too highly aggregated, but selection of the proper level of aggregation for the base data makes promotional analysis much more straightforward.

Sales Measurement

Sales are traditionally presented in the form of market share in marketing plans. A *market share* is simply the sales for a given product brand divided by the total sales in the product category. A market share is a good way of comparing the performance of an individual brand against competing brands. This is why it is so often used as a means of expressing product sales. When used at high levels of data aggregation such as annual U.S. sales volume, it is a good indication of relative effectiveness.

A problem in using market share for short run analysis is that competitive activity is included in the number. For example, if brand A runs a promotion and enjoys an increase in sales, and if brand B also runs a promotion at the same time and increases sales, brand A may have very little change in market share, but may register significant volume sales increases. Because market share also includes competitive activity, market share loses sensitivity to a given sales promotion program.

A much better measure of sales to evaluate sales promotion is then *sales volume* and not market share. This principle is also demonstrated in the cases that follow. A second problem with market share is that an accurate assessment is required as to which brands or products constitute the appropriate market. Many product categories such as sliced lunch meats, canned soups, salted snacks, cookies, and snack crackers have a large variety of sizes, forms, and flavors. Improper specification of the items to be used as a basis for market share may materially bias analyses.

Financial Analysis

The appropriate framework for evaluating sales promotion programs is the income statement, which allows direct comparison of profit levels. The income statement can also provide a most convenient planning tool as well as means of evaluation.

Income Statements

The income statement is perhaps the most fundamental of all financial statements. The income statement is sometimes referred to as a profit or loss statement. It shows the relationship among sales, costs, and profits. A sales promotion program, whether it be offered by a manufacturer or a retailer, should have impact on both the sales and the costs and, of course, the profit.

A simplified statement (Table 2-1) shows the relationship between the manufacturer and retailer and the source of promotional expenses. The manufacturer incurs costs with the trade allowances and in promotional expenses, and the retailer in promotional expenses.

Table 2-1
INCOME STATEMENT

Manufacturer	Retailer
Gross Sales	Gross Sales
— Discounts and Adjustments	— Returns
— Trade Allowances*	
	Net Sales
Net Sales	— Cost of Goods
— Cost of Goods	
— Warehouse and Freight	Gross Margin
— Brokerage Fees	— Retailer Promotion*
	— Other Expenses
Contribution to Margin	
— Manufacturer Promotion*	Retailer Profit
— Other Expenses	
Manufacturer Profit	

*Promotional Expenses

As discussed previously, the expense categories each contain both fixed and variable components which need to be recognized in order to be able to determine profit. The above model simplifies the distribution channel somewhat in that warehouses and brokers are recognized as costs to the manufacturer. Certainly promotion is possible to middlemen, but most of the trade promotion in this book will be assumed to be aimed at retailers.

Financial Forecasts

The format of the income statement can be readily applied as both a tool to evaluate a past sales promotion program as well as a means to forecast the effect of a future program. By comparing income statements for successive time intervals, past sales promotion programs can be evaluated by comparing the intervals when the promotion was present to those intervals when the promotion was not.

The difficulty in comparing many time intervals is performing the repetitious computations that are necessary. This is easily solved with a microcomputer with a spread sheet program. Such a program makes the repetitious computations as simple as representing the relationship between rows and columns in terms of simple algebra. Almost any of the currently commercially available spread sheet programs can be adapted to this purpose.

Once the appropriate historical data have been entered, it is then a simple matter to perform the computations with a spread sheet program. The appropriate comparisons can be made, followed by the strategic promotional decisions. The microcomputer model can also be used as a forecasting tool, allowing the asking of fanciful "what if" questions. The analyst can enter projected values for future time periods, make reasonable assumptions from the historical data, and evaluate potential sales promotion programs. This, of course, could be done manually, but it would take a considerable amount of time.

Forward Buying

Many sales promotion programs involve the shifting of purchase patterns in time. Analyzing purchase timing requires that special attention be paid to the time periods before, during, and after the promotional period.

A manufacturer may announce a new allowance and promotional program to the trade. The trade may also anticipate a promotional program from a manufacturer because of their experience during previous years. The trade would be expected then to defer purchase of the product from the manufacturer until the special promotional price is available. The trade would also be expected to purchase more of the product than they normally would, to take advantage of the special price in anticipation of future sales to consumers. This phenomenon is known as forward buying. Presumably, after the promotional period, then the trade demand for the product would diminish until the additional quantity that was purchased during the promotion was sold.

From the point of view of the manufacturer, forward buying moves quantity of the product from inventory and may result in incremental sales volume gain. From the point of view of the retailer, it affords an opportunity to obtain the product at a lower price, although this needs to be carefully balanced against inventory holding costs and lowered selling prices and margins.

Time Series Analysis

Analyzing data across successive time periods, or a *time series*, is one of the best ways to generalize from historical data. Sales data are naturally arrayed in a temporal sequence. One of the most common ways of analyzing time series data is linear regression, although several special problems need to be considered.

Linear Regression

A detailed discussion of linear regression can be found in any of several books dealing with statistics. In general, *linear regression* is a way of establishing a linear algebraic relationship between a criterion or dependent variable and one or more predictor or independent variables. The equation is in the form $Y=a+bX$, where Y is the criterion variable and X is the predictor variable. The *criterion variable* is the variable that is to be estimated, such as sales or profit. The *predictor variable* or variables are the variables that are presumed to influence the criterion variable, such as the presence or absence of a sales promotion program. In the equation, the "a" is referred to as the *intercept* and the "b" as the *slope*, or the relative change in Y that is attributable to X. The slope is also commonly referred to as the *regression coefficient*.

Linear regression is an extremely useful tool for accounting for differences in a time series. The relationship, however, is limited to a straight line. If the data points in the series were plotted on a graph, they would no doubt not form a very good straight line. This raises the issue of fitting the best possible line through the data points. The most common method for accomplishing this is the method of *least squares*, or the line fit that is the line that has the smallest sum of the squared distances between the actual data points and the points along the theoretical line. Sometimes this method is referred to as *ordinary least squares*.

Several computer software packages are available that are capable of performing analyses of this type. Obviously the appropriate manual should be consulted, as well as other books on the interpretation and application of linear regression. There are some special considerations in analyzing the data appropriate to scanner based data.

Coding Variables

Linear regression has some reasonably stringent requirements for variables that can be included as either predictor variables, such as promotional conditions, or criterion variables, such as sales. Variables must be measured at least at the interval level, meaning that nominal or categorical variables are generally excluded. This means that the variable itself must be measured on a scale similar to a temperature scale with the degrees representing equal scale intervals. Variables, such as sales and price, can usually be assumed to be interval variables.

Other variables, such as the presence or absence of a particular promotion, or an in-store display, or an advertised price, cannot be assumed to be interval variables. The solution is the *dummy coded variable*, or the "0-1" variable. For those time periods when the promotion is present, a predictor variable is created that is coded a "1." When the promotion is not present, the same variable is coded as a "0." This same method can be applied to a whole host of predictor variables that might have some relationship to sales, such as the day of the week or the season.

Experiments

By coding the presence of a sales promotion program using dummy variables, historical data can be analyzed as though an experiment were conducted. The control condition becomes all of those times when the promotion is not present or the dummy variable is coded "0." The non-promotion times become the "base business" for the particular brand and are the average business or sales for the non-promotion times. Particular care must be taken if one effect of the promotion is to cause inventory stockpiling by retailer or consumers. In this case, base sales may be artificially depressed during periods following a promotion.

While the analysis has been described here as similar to an experiment, it is not a true experiment in the strict sense. The control and experimental conditions are not strictly parallel in time, and it is always possible that the time of the promotion condition was unusual in some way, making it different from the average of other times. This can be partially solved by conducting experiments in different markets at different points in time. Certainly the analyst needs to be aware of the issue.

Autoregression

A particularly difficult problem with any time series analysis is the potential for autoregression. *Autoregression* means self-correlated. A variable, such as sales, is not independent across the successive time intervals. In other words, sales in this time period are influenced by sales in the prior time period because of such considerations as the size of the business, distribution, or reputation. A large retailer or manufacturer is not expected to experience dramatic total sales fluctuations, although individual line items may have large swings. In the absence of promotional activity, item sales in any given week will be about the same as sales of the item in the previous week, perhaps with trends and seasonal adjustments.

The problem with autoregression is that it can substantially distort the regression equation. It normally makes the strength of the relationship between the variables appear stronger than it actually is. This might give the analyst an illusion of false knowledge and lead to possible overconfidence in the estimation of the impact of a sales promotion program. The most serious problem occurs when the error (difference between actual and estimate from regression equation) exhibits autoregression.

The problem of autoregression is a major topic in any course in econometrics. Certainly the analyst needs to be aware of the potential of the problem. The appropriate statistical test, such as Durbin-Watson, should be run to determine whether or not autoregression is a problem. If it does exist, then some method, such as first differences, should be used to eliminate or control the problem. One of the many books on econometrics provides the necessary details, as well as the manuals for the statistical software packages. A reference list is provided at the end of the chapter.

Case: Salad Seasoning

The Wondo Company has the problem of establishing the wholesale and retail price of one of their products, salad seasoning. The Wondo Company is currently marketing a very successful product that is well-known by consumers throughout the country.

Background   Wondo has conducted price testing for the product at retail prices of $1.24, $1.44, and $1.64 per unit. This product is generally priced by the retailers at cost plus 20 percent, so that a manufacturer list price of $1.20 per unit will translate to a retail shelf price of $1.44. The retailers have a preference for psychological pricing, and tend to use prices that end in 4 or 9, and will adjust prices after mark-up to the closest such price point. The Wondo Company management believes that no change in the wholesale price should be made which would result in retail prices lower than $1.24 per unit, or higher than $1.64 per unit.

The Wondo Company conducted a national sales test manipulating the retail prices. Estimates from the test indicate that the national sales expected at various retail price levels are as follows:

Retail Price Per Unit	Annual Unit Sales
$1.24	13,000,000
$1.44	10,000,000
$1.64	7,000,000

The current national price for the product is $1.44. The decision facing Wondo management is whether or not this price should be changed.

A typical retailer must also be considered in this situation. A typical retailer, a supermarket chain with several stores, operates with a 20 percent mark-up rule. The chain income statement is as follows:

Total Annual Sales	$60,000,000 (All Commodities)
Cost of Goods	50,000,000
Gross Margin	10,000,000
Fixed Operating Cost	2,500,000
Variable Operating Cost	6,250,000
Gross Profit	1,250,000

The normal level of sales of the Wondo Company product for this retailer are 500 units per week when it is priced at $1.44.

Question 1 The Wondo Company is considering a change in the base retail price. The possibilities being considered are as follows:

Wholesale	Estimated Retail
$1.04	$1.24
1.08	1.29
1.12	1.34
1.16	1.39
1.20	1.44
1.24	1.49
1.28	1.54
1.32	1.59
1.36	1.64

Part 1: Suppose that the cost elements for the Wondo Company are $7,000,000 in fixed operating costs and 30¢ variable cost per unit. Plot the estimated gross profit for the Wondo Company at the various wholesale prices. What price would yield maximum profit?
Part 2: Suppose that the cost elements for the Wondo Company are $3,000,000 in fixed operating costs and 70¢ variable cost per unit. Plot the estimated gross profit for the Wondo Company at the various wholesale prices. What price would yield maximum profit?

Question 2 The retailer in this case might want to consider using a profit maximization rule rather than a simple mark-up rule to determine the retail price. Assume that the cost elements for the Wondo Company are $7,000,000 in fixed operating cost, 30¢ in variable costs per unit, and the wholesale selling price is $1.20. If the 20 percent mark-up rule is used, the typical retailer would charge $1.44.

Suppose, however, that the sales response for the retailer parallels the national estimates, which the retailer has determined through research. The retailer also estimates that the variable operating costs for the Wondo product are about the same as the average for the entire chain. Plot the estimated contribution to retailer profit and fixed costs over the range of retail prices from $1.24 to $1.64. What action would you recommend to the retailer?

Question 3 There is a natural tug-of-war that exists between the manufacturer and the retailer. Assume that the Wondo Company assumptions are the same as in

Question 2, and that all retailers behave in the same way as the chain previously described.

Part 1: Suppose that all retailers are profit maximizers. For the range of wholesale prices considered in Question 1, what would be the expected retail prices and resulting annual sales volumes of the Wondo Company product? Plot the contribution to profit and fixed costs for:

• The Wondo Company
• All retailers
• Wondo and the retailers combined.

Part 2: Redo Part 1 assuming that all retailers operate on the 20 percent mark-up rule.

Question 4   This question deals with the retailers' response to a trade price discount. Again assume that the cost characteristics for the Wondo Company are the same as they are in Question 2 and the wholesale price is $1.20. Assume that all retailers operate on a 20 percent mark-up rule. Retailers also normally order a two-week supply once every two weeks, and they incur a carrying inventory cost of 1 percent of the purchase price per unit cost per week.

The Wondo Company wishes to boost fourth-quarter volume, which has been lagging. The following offer is made to all retailers: During the last two weeks of the fourth quarter, each retailer can place an order for up to 12 times its normal weekly level of sales. The price charged will be $1.00 versus the normal $1.20. Delivery will be on the first day of the next quarter.

Assume that all sales over the amount expected for 13 weeks of regular pricing are incremental to the brand, and not the result of forward buying by the consumer. In other words, the consumer will use more of the product rather than stockpile it.

Part 1: Estimate the probable size of the order from a retailer who intends to maintain the base shelf price of $1.44, increasing profit through increased margin. (HINT: Develop an algebraic equation.)

Part 2: Estimate the probable size of the order from a retailer who intends to pass through the savings directly to consumers by reducing shelf price to $1.24 while the supply lasts.

Part 3: Making whatever assumptions you feel are necessary, estimate the sales of the product by the manufacturer during the two weeks of the offer and the 13 weeks of the next quarter if:

• All retailers maintain shelf price
• All retailers reduce price to $1.24

Part 4: Discuss the advantages and disadvantages to the Wondo Company that might be associated with this offer.

Part 5: The retailer has other options besides no pass-through and complete pass-through of the temporary price reduction. To reduce the store margin, the retailer might opt for partial pass-through in addition to the manufacturer's reduction in order to provide an extremely attractive shelf price. Assume that once the supply of specially priced product is exhausted, regular pricing of $1.44 is resumed. Plot the expected contribution to retailer profit and fixed costs for the 13 weeks following receipt of the order versus alternative pricing points.

3 *Consumer Response to Sales Promotion*

Measuring consumer response to sales promotion has always been a difficult task. Until the availability of scanner data, measuring consumer response was limited to aggregate summarizing of coupon redemptions, estimates of monthly or bimonthly sales volume, and consumer attitude surveys, or conducting expensive experimentation. After scanner data became readily available, actual consumer shopping behavior was capable of being easily analyzed. For products sold in grocery outlets, both the product brand must be considered, and the store itself, since not only is loyalty to a brand important, but also loyalty to a store. Additionally, the mix of items offered in a category may vary dramatically from store to store. Particularly important may be the presence of private label or store brands, and generic products.

Store Shopping Loyalty

The average consumer visits between three and four stores in a 12-week period according to a 1984 IRI study of 10,000 households. Only 8 percent of all consumers shop in exclusively one store during the same period, and 26 percent shop in five or more stores. Obviously the majority of shoppers visit more than one store. (See Figure 3-1.)

Figure 3-1

NUMBER OF STORES VISITED IN 12 WEEKS

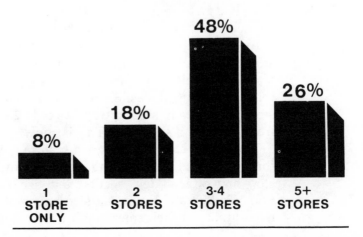

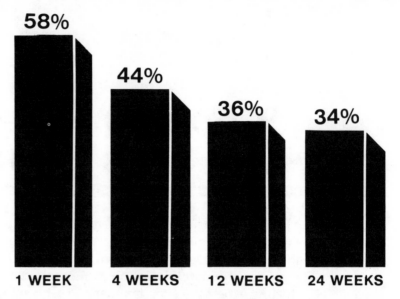

Figure 3-2

ARE SHOPPERS LOYAL TO A SINGLE STORE?*

58%

44%

36%

34%

| 1 WEEK | 4 WEEKS | 12 WEEKS | 24 WEEKS |

* Percent Giving 85% or More of Business to a Single Store

Recognition that shoppers visit more than one store in a three-month period raises the question of whether or not they give all the stores an equal amount of business. Examining store loyalty shows that they don't. Using 85 percent or more of the business to a single store as the criteria for loyalty, 58 percent of all shoppers are loyal to a single store in a one-week period. This drops to 36 percent in a 12-week period and doesn't change very much even over 24 weeks as shown in Figure 3-2. It seems that about one-third of all shoppers are loyal to a single store regardless of the time period. This loyalty, however, does not mean that they do not visit other stores. It means that some shoppers tend to do most of their shopping in one store.

Store Characteristics

While there are many ways of classifying retail grocery outlets, one good way is weekly or annual dollar sales volume. Stores can be arranged according to their sales volume into three groups. From a 1984 IRI study, stores in the top third had an average weekly dollar sales volume of $255,000; the middle third, $143,000; and the bottom third, $63,000.

As might be expected, the average store loyalty changes with the size of the store. The largest stores, or the top store group, enjoy 37 percent of the total store dollar volume from store loyal shoppers. Again, loyal shoppers are those that are making at least 85 percent of their dollar volume in purchases at one store. The bottom store group has only 28.5 percent of the total store volume from store loyal shoppers. This is shown in Figure 3-3.

The largest stores enjoy greater store loyalty than the smaller stores. Often this is achieved by providing a greater range of goods and services. The large store may offer a "deli" section, a house plant section, and an extensive selection of health and beauty aids and general merchandise items. Smaller stores obtain more of their sales volume from shoppers who are not loyal. The dif-

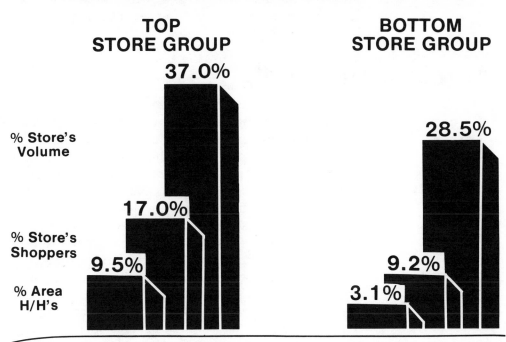

Figure 3-3

HOW IMPORTANT ARE LOYAL BUYERS?

TOP STORE GROUP

37.0%

% Store's Volume

17.0%

% Store's Shoppers

9.5%

% Area H/H's

BOTTOM STORE GROUP

28.5%

9.2%

3.1%

ference between the largest and the smallest stores widens if the stores' shopper counts, rather than sales volume, are used for comparison.

Importance of Promotion

One way of assessing the importance of sales promotion by the type of store is to examine the purchases made with a special price or deal. As might be expected, as a shopper visits more stores, more purchases are made on deal. Figure 3-4 shows the relationship between the number of stores visited and the proportion of purchases made on deal. Indexing the one or two store visit

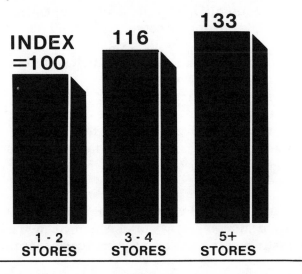

Figure 3-4

IMPORTANCE OF PROMOTION BY NUMBER OF STORES VISITED
(Indexed % Purchase on Deal)

133

INDEX =100

116

| 1 - 2 STORES | 3 - 4 STORES | 5+ STORES |

category at 100, those visiting five or more stores are making 33 percent more purchases on deal. Clearly price promotions seem to be related to store visits, although this does not necessarily mean that they are building store loyalty. Some shoppers may be visiting several chains weekly to take advantage of promotional prices.

Brand Shopping Loyalty

Beyond loyalty to a store, there is also loyalty to individual brands found in the store. The issue of brand loyalty seems to be critical in determining the impact of promotion, especially price promotions.

The first critical problem for the manufacturer is to understand whether the particular brand is price sensitive or promotion responsive, or both. To determine that, the following questions need attention: How does the particular brand respond when offered on deal? How does the product respond to non-promoted base price changes? What happens to the product category when the brand is promoted? What happens to the brand when the deal ends? Does high brand loyalty mean that the brand is promotion responsive?

How a brand responds to competitive price and promotion is also critical in understanding that brand. High brand loyalty should protect a brand from sales loss to competitive promotions. If a brand is very price sensitive, then a competitive promotion should be successful in converting sales away from the brand, and everyday price levels are also critically important.

Another problem is to understand whether a promotion results in stockpiling by current brand users, or in obtaining incremental sales from switchers that buy primarily on deal from a set of several equally acceptable brands. Understanding the brand loyalty is critical to understanding the sales performance of the brand and the potential role that can be played by promotion.

Brand Switching
A typical brand sold through grocery retail stores can divide the source of its business into five categories. Usually the largest category is switchers, those product category purchasers who purchase less than 70 percent to 80 percent of any one brand in the long run from the category. In contrast, most manufacturers would like the largest category to be purchasers who are exclusively loyal to the brand. A second loyal category is those who don't purchase the brand exclusively, but do purchase the brand at least 70 percent to 80 percent of the time. The two remaining categories consist of those purchasers who are loyal to another brand at least 70 percent to 80 percent of the time, and those who are infrequent category purchasers. Infrequent category purchasers have not made enough purchases to be categorized as brand loyal buyers or as brand switchers.

Figure 3-5 shows a typical brand, "Brand A," with the source of business by loyalty type. Of interest is the comparison between a non-promoted week and a promoted week. Overall sales for the brand increased 136 percent during the promoted week. By far the largest increase is shown in the switcher category although all categories show some increase.

Cherry Picking
A relatively new phenomenon is observable among scanner-based panel studies of shopping behavior; it is termed cherry picking. *Cherry picking* is an interesting side effect of the increased emphasis on promotion. This

Figure 3-5

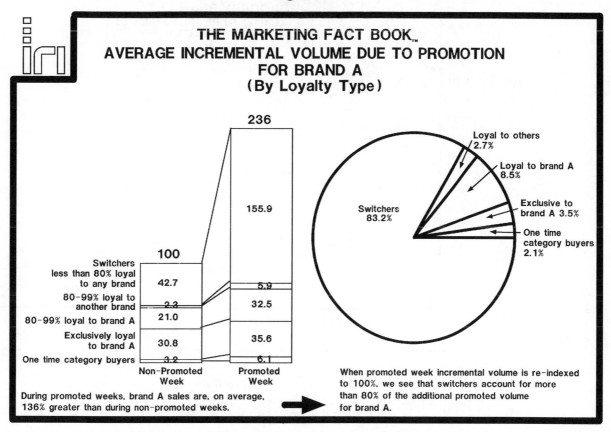

THE MARKETING FACT BOOK™
AVERAGE INCREMENTAL VOLUME DUE TO PROMOTION
FOR BRAND A
(By Loyalty Type)

During promoted weeks, brand A sales are, on average, 136% greater than during non-promoted weeks.

When promoted week incremental volume is re-indexed to 100%, we see that switchers account for more than 80% of the additional promoted volume for brand A.

phenomenon is characterized by shoppers who nearly always buy the brand that is offered on deal. This particular phenomenon has been created by the proliferation of promotion and the training of the shoppers to wait for the next promotion that they know is coming.

The cherry picker is not the same as the shopper who is motivated entirely by price. The lowest possible price, such as might be found with private brands and generics, is not necessarily the objective of the cherry picker. Rather, it is the best deal among a set of acceptable brands. The cherry picker may well defer purchase until a deal is offered, and may also conversely stockpile. In product categories that are heavily promoted and frequently purchased, the cherry picker may be even brand loyal. In colas, for example, there are shoppers who will only buy one brand when it is offered with a deal, shopping multiple stores to maximize exposure to deals.

Price Sensitivity

It is critically important to understand the relationship between selling price and sales volume for both the product category and the brand before any price promotion is applied. In general the relationship would be expected to follow a downward sloping curve as is normally depicted in typical demand curves.

The curve shown in Figure 3-6 shows typical demand curves for "Brand A"

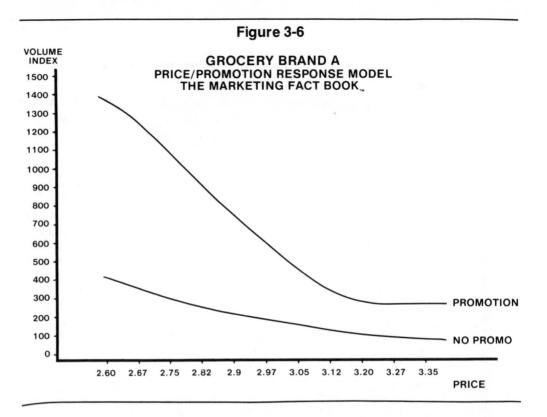

Figure 3-6

GROCERY BRAND A
PRICE/PROMOTION RESPONSE MODEL
THE MARKETING FACT BOOK™

for conditions both of when a price promotion is in effect and when there is no promotion. The no promotion curve clearly shows increasing sales volume as the price decreases. The promotion curve shows an even stronger relationship, except at the higher prices, or at very low prices where a saturation effect is observed. This price curve is based on the assumption of no competitive price changes.

The change in direction of the promotion curve near the $3.20 price shows a potentially serious problem. A demand curve that changes direction is commonly referred to as being kinked. A *kinked demand curve* means that a change in price does not change the volume. In other words, promotional prices between approximately $3.20 and $3.35 yield approximately the same sales volume. Reducing prices below the current $3.20 yields sharply increased promotional sales volume. At promotion prices below $2.60, little additional sales are gained.

If the demand curve is kinked for a particular product category or brand, it is critically important for the manager to know the promotional response function. Price discounts below the saturation level only depress sales revenue. In actual practice, most of the product categories that are sold through grocery retail outlets that have been studied have kinked demand curves. That makes performance of the type of analysis suggested here especially important.

Promotion Responsiveness

Not only does the price make a difference in the quantity of the product sold, but also important is the presence or absence of both in-store displays and store feature advertising. The price/promotion response model shown in Figure 3-7 represents percent changes in sales volume with percent price

Figure 3-7

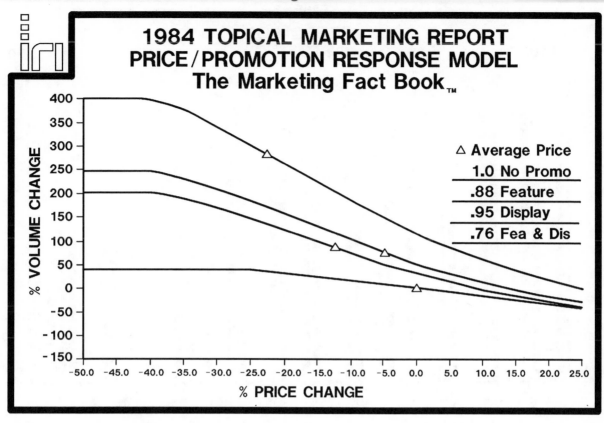

changes for four conditions: no promotion activity, only store feature advertising activity, only in-store display activity, and both feature advertising and in-store displays. This chart is an aggregate of many product categories sold in grocery stores and does not reflect any particular product category or brand characteristics.

Without any change in price, feature advertising and in-store displays often increase sales volume. As shown in the figure, in-store displays by themselves usually increase sales volume in most product categories slightly more than does feature advertising by itself. Most important here is that both together increase incremental sales volume nearly as much as each operating alone. Features and displays have a strong synergistic effect with price. When price reductions are combined with in-store displays and feature advertising, sales volume can increase by as much as 400 percent, whereas a price reduction alone can only yield about a 40 percent volume increase.

Post-Promotion Sales Declines

Common sense would suggest that dramatic sales increases during a price promotion would be followed by at least a short period of sales decline. The actual sales data for most retail outlets, however, show little post-promotion sales decline.

Figure 3-8 shows a typical example for 16-ounce Pepsi. The dotted line shows the selling price as represented on the right axis. The solid line shows

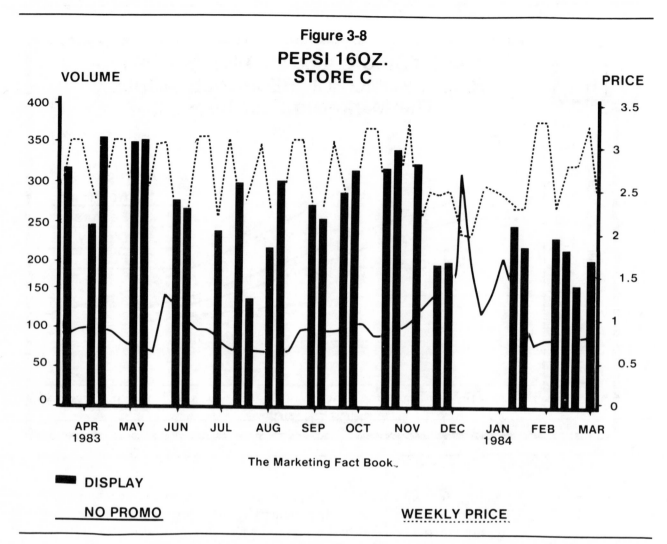

Figure 3-8

PEPSI 16OZ. STORE C

VOLUME   PRICE

The Marketing Fact Book...

■ DISPLAY

NO PROMO   WEEKLY PRICE

the sales volume as represented by the axis on the left. Promotions are represented by the vertical bars. In the first week shown, for example, sales were in excess of 300 units in "Store C" with a display promotion. In the second week, with no promotion, sales fell back to approximately 100 units.

Of interest is that, during most of the promotion periods, sales increase dramatically from the sales during the non-promotion periods. The post-promotion periods do not appear to be less than the period just prior to the promotion. In fact, sometimes the non-promotion sales increase after the promotion ends. Figure 3-5 indicates the reason. For most promotions the incremental volume is coming from switchers who do not purchase during non-promotional periods. Only when loyal buyers are stockpiling is the product purchased on promotion.

Pepsi in the 16-ounce size is one of the most heavily promoted products in the store. The relationship still holds true in a much less frequently promoted package size, Pepsi in the 2-liter size. Figure 3-9 can be interpreted in the same way as the previous chart. It is important to notice that there is no large dip in sales following a promotion. Current research suggests that the dip, if it exists, is shallow and occurs over a long time. The result is that the baseline may be artificially low, particularly if deals occur frequently. Perhaps equally important is that there does not seem to be an increase in sales following a

Figure 3-9

PEPSI 2 LITER
STORE A

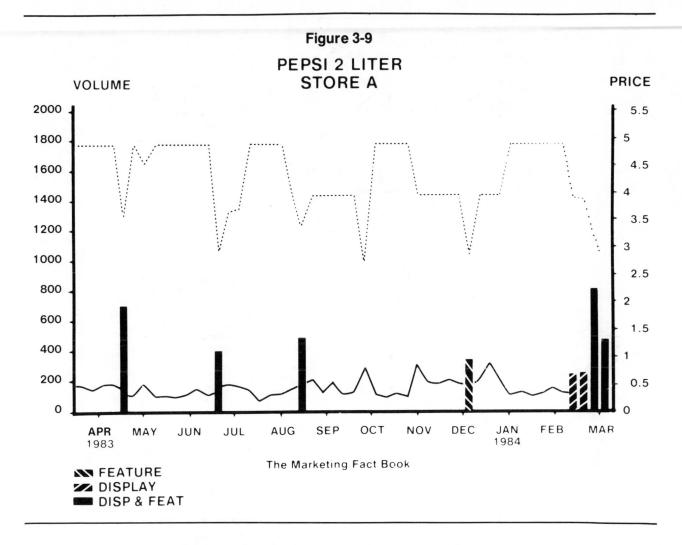

VOLUME

PRICE

FEATURE
DISPLAY
DISP & FEAT

The Marketing Fact Book

promotion either. This again reinforces the point that sales promotion must be evaluated during the same period that the promotion occurs. In other words, the promotion will generate immediate sales, but will not necessarily generate any future business after the promotion.

For the manufacturer, promotions may have quite a different effect on shipments. The manufacturer typically offers promotion to the trade from two to six times per year. Retailers must purchase sufficient product to minimize chances of running out of stock when the promotion is passed through to consumers. In addition, the reduced price from the manufacturer may justify stockpiling purchases by the retailer. For example, suppose the manufacturer offers a promotional incentive to the retailer which when passed through and given advertising feature support would result in a sales increase of about three weeks extra business. Due to local variability, retailers know that 95 percent of the time, the actual sales will be between one week extra and five weeks extra. Further, at this price, it is worthwhile to stockpile two weeks worth of business. The retailer who wishes to minimize out-of-stocks and have stockpiled inventory might then place an order for eight weeks worth of regular sales instead of one week's worth. The manufacturer then sees a total shipment of eight weeks regular sales volume, which represents from the retailer one week regular volume, three weeks incremental volume, and four

Figure 3-10

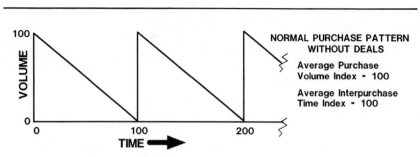

NORMAL PURCHASE PATTERN WITHOUT DEALS

Average Purchase Volume Index - 100

Average Interpurchase Time Index - 100

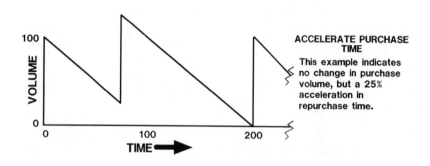

ACCELERATE PURCHASE TIME

This example indicates no change in purchase volume, but a 25% acceleration in repurchase time.

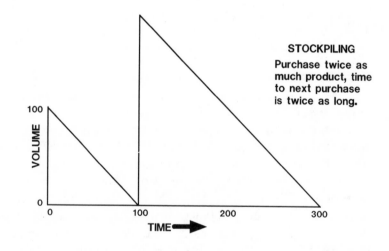

STOCKPILING

Purchase twice as much product, time to next purchase is twice as long.

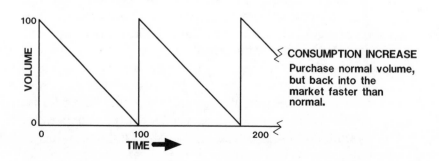

CONSUMPTION INCREASE

Purchase normal volume, but back into the market faster than normal.

weeks safety stock and stockpiling. The manufacturer will suffer in the future a depression of about four weeks worth of sales to such a retailer.

Purchase Timing

A commonly discussed impact of sales promotion is the alteration of the purchase cycle. Of course to consider any alteration of the purchase cycle, it is first necessary to be able to describe it. Figure 3-10 shows how purchase timing can be quantitatively described.

The normal purchase pattern without any deals is shown at the top with the average purchase volume indexed to 100 and the average inter-purchase time indexed to 100. This provides a symmetrical representation of the normal purchase cycle. It is now relatively easy to distinguish alterations in purchase timing.

Accelerating purchase time is shown in the second pattern, and indicates no increase in purchase volume, but a decrease in the repurchase time. The chart shows an example of a 25 percent acceleration in repurchase time.

The third pattern is stockpiling, which is purchasing more quantity and increasing the repurchase time appropriately. The chart shows an example of purchasing twice as much and then stretching the repurchase time to twice as long.

The last pattern, a consumption increase, shows the normal volume purchased on each occasion, but the repurchase time decreased so that the consumer is back into the market faster than normal.

Using canned tuna as an example, an IRI study of purchase timing effects over 80 weeks in eight markets provides some interesting insight into the relationship between promotion and purchase timing. The particular characteristics of the tuna category are shown in Figure 3-11. Aggregate tuna purchasing behavior is shown for the 80 weeks. Annual tuna sales per 1,000 households

Figure 3-11

DATA BASE
TUNA CATEGORY PURCHASING
THE MARKETING FACT BOOK™

- 80 Weeks 2/6/84 - 8/18/85
- 8 Cities
- 14,624 Households
- 13,579 Category Buyers
- 177,959 Purchases of Canned Tuna
- $248,231 Spending

City	Annual Tuna Sales Per 1000 Households	Average Price Per Pound	% Volume Sold With Promotion
1	10.7	$1.73	68%
2	4.0	1.74	42
3	5.7	1.71	51
4	5.6	2.07	46
5	4.9	1.83	51
6	6.5	1.93	23
7	5.9	1.94	46
8	5.3	1.82	40

ranged from 10.7 pounds to 4 pounds in the 8 markets, and the volume sold with promotion ranged from 23 percent to 68 percent.

Using a regression analysis on scanner panel households who are in the most sensitive market segment to promotional activity—the non-loyal deal sensitive segment described previously in this chapter—tuna sales are analyzed according to the volume of the product sold on deal, the usage characteristics of the household, and the purchase timing. The proportion of total market sales on deal is divided into three categories: light (23 percent),

Figure 3-12

MODEL ESTIMATES
NON-LOYAL DEAL SENSITIVE MODEL

Trade Deal Only
Average Purchase Size Index

By % Market Volume Sold On Deal	By Average Volume In 80 Weeks		
	2#	8#	32#
23%	79	166.9	351
46%	67	109	176
69%	61	85	118

Figure 3-13

MODEL ESTIMATES
NON-LOYAL DEAL SENSITIVE MODEL

Trade Deal Only
Purchase Cycle Change
(In Index Points)

By % Market Volume Sold On Deal	By Average Volume In Pounds		
	2#	8#	32#
23%	+46.2	+34.2	+18.5
46%	+19.8	+3.5	-13.8
69%	+5.0	-10.6	-24.8

medium (46 percent), and heavy (68 percent).

Product usage is also divided into three groups: light, who purchase an average of 2 pounds in 80 weeks; medium, who purchase an average of 8 pounds in 80 weeks; and heavy, who purchase an average of 32 pounds in 80 weeks. Figure 3-12 shows the relative volume changes when a deal is present. When there has been little volume sold on deal, and a deal is present, the heavy users (32 pounds) will increase their average volume by 351 percent. As the proportion of the volume sold on deal increases, so does the average purchase size. This clearly indicates an anticipation effect; if the consumer sees the product being promoted regularly, a new promotion seems to be considerably less effective.

Figure 3-13, from a regression model, represents only the incremental impact due to the particular timing change described. Other effects would, in effect, be held constant. In other words, an individual household may be accelerating purchase and increasing consumption at the same time. The following tables then show the relative impact for each timing effect alone, holding the others constant.

Purchase acceleration from the tuna example is clearly evident, but it diminishes dramatically as the proportion of the volume sold on deal increases. At the highest level of deal activity, the purchase timing is actually slowed. The greatest volume changes in terms of purchase acceleration seem to be from the light and medium users. The relative effect on heavy users is relatively small.

Stockpiling is shown as an effect across the board but is especially strong when the deal volume is light among heavy users. When deal volume is high, heavy users are slightly less likely to stockpile as shown in Figure 3-14. In terms of stockpiling, light users seem indifferent to the proportion of the volume sold on deal.

Figure 3-14

MODEL ESTIMATES
NON-LOYAL DEAL SENSITIVE MODEL

Trade Deal Only
Stockpiling
(In Index Points)

By % Market Volume Sold On Deal	By Average Volume In 80 Weeks		
	2#	8#	32#
23%	+15.4	+52.3	+124.4
46%	+14.3	+22.3	+ 29.8
69%	+13.4	3.7	- 5

Figure 3-15

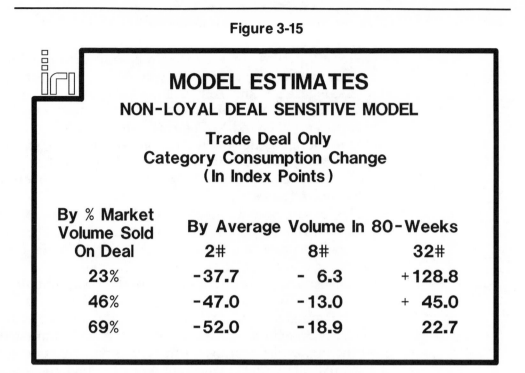

MODEL ESTIMATES

NON-LOYAL DEAL SENSITIVE MODEL

Trade Deal Only
Category Consumption Change
(In Index Points)

By % Market Volume Sold On Deal	By Average Volume In 80-Weeks		
	2#	8#	32#
23%	-37.7	- 6.3	+128.8
46%	-47.0	-13.0	+ 45.0
69%	-52.0	-18.9	22.7

Figure 3-16

QUARTERLY PEPSI SALES BY PACKAGE SIZE
MARKET A

100 POINTS

7000

6000

5000

4000

3000

2000

1000

0

2 LITER BOTTLES   16OZ. BOTTLES   12OZ. CANS

■ FEB – APR
■ MAY – JUL
■ AUG – OCT
▦ NOV – JAN

Figure 3-17

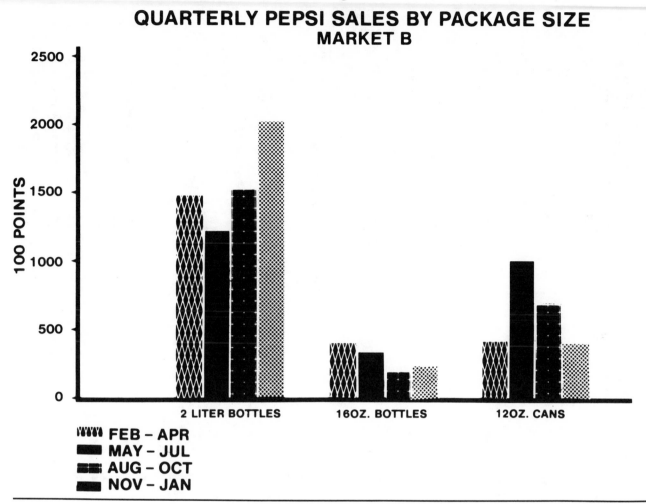

QUARTERLY PEPSI SALES BY PACKAGE SIZE
MARKET B

Only heavy users seem to be encouraged to increase their category consumption because of the presence of a promotion. The effect, as shown in Figure 3-15, is clearly related to the proportion of the volume sold on deal. Light and medium users appear to decrease their category consumption, indicating that their deal purchases may be planned for long periods of time, while their purchases of tuna at regular price are more need-driven.

Effects of Package Size

Beyond the store and the brand, another important factor is the effect of package size. Different shoppers purchase different package sizes, and promotion of the wrong size might lead to failure. Hence, the package size must be considered along with the product category and brand.

Figure 3-16 shows the quarterly sales of Pepsi in Market A for three package sizes: 2-liter bottles, 16-ounce bottles, and 12-ounce cans. Market A shows a strong preference for 16-ounce bottles.

Not all markets, however, favor the same package size as Market A. Figure 3-17 shows quarterly Pepsi sales by package size for Market B. Market B seems to favor the 2-liter bottle, while the 16-ounce bottle drops to last place in popularity. A promotion of 16-ounce bottles would no doubt have differential im-

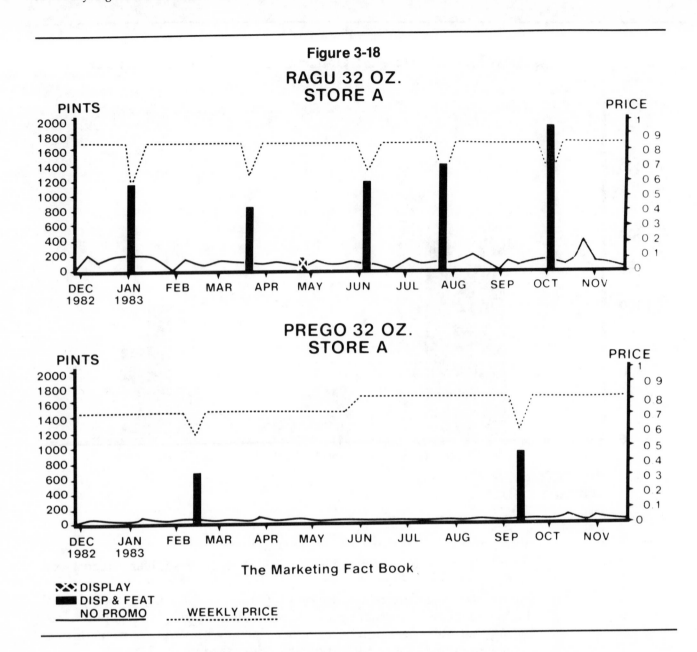

Figure 3-18

**RAGU 32 OZ.
STORE A**

**PREGO 32 OZ.
STORE A**

The Marketing Fact Book

⬛⬛ DISPLAY
⬛ DISP & FEAT
NO PROMO   .... WEEKLY PRICE

pact in Market A versus Market B. Certainly one promotion function does not fit all market situations or brand sizes.

Effects on Competitive Products

Common sense would again seem to say that when a brand is sold with a price promotion, competitive brands should suffer lessened sales. Presumably as the brand that is promoted increases its sales volume, it takes sales from the competitors.

The actual data, however, show that competitive brands seldom have major sales declines during the promotional periods of other brands. On the contrary, sometimes competitive brands enjoy sales increases.

A typical pattern can be seen in the spaghetti sauce product category. Figure 3-18 compares the sales and promotion in Store A for Ragu and Prego in the same size package. Both brands have fairly stable prices. Prego raised its price in June. At the same time, Ragu used more promotion, running six retail promotions compared to Prego's two. The important point is that when Ragu runs a promotion, it seems to have very little impact on Prego volume, and vice versa. Exceptions are the Prego promotions during February and September when the Ragu sales volume appears to increase slightly.

In general, the effects on competitive sales are minimal, while the primary effect is one on the brand that is promoted during the period of that promotion. The sales responses illustrate again the impact of having a majority of incremental sales promotion response due to switchers who do not show up in the base. Over time, if both brands were to dramatically cut back on promotions, the switchers might surface in the base line sales. Conversely, increasing promotional frequency might switch more households out of the base and into a promotion-only buying pattern.

Long-Term Effects

It is clear that promotion generates short-term effects, but the long-term effects are less obvious. Can sales promotion help to create long-term base-level business?

Base-level business is the sales level that a brand has during non-

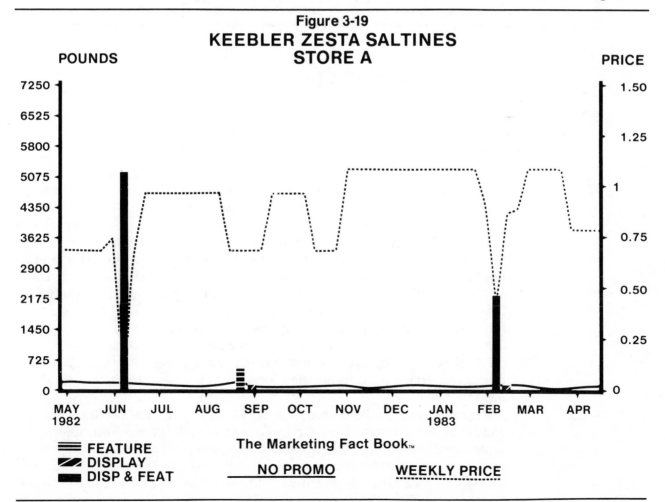

Figure 3-19
KEEBLER ZESTA SALTINES
STORE A

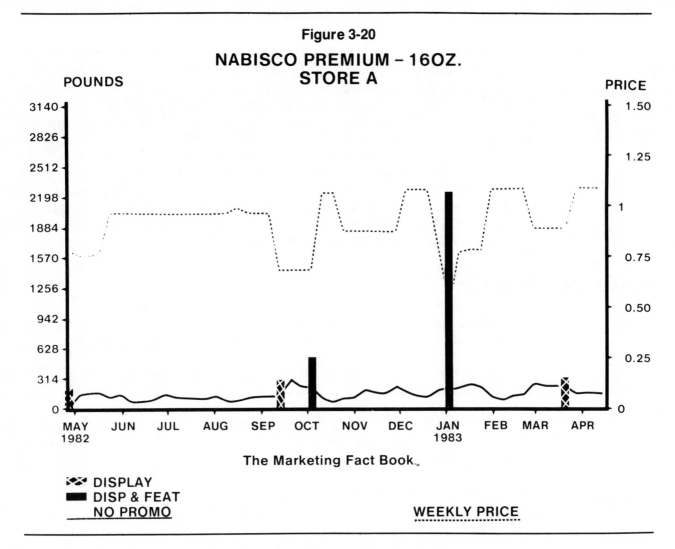

Figure 3-20
NABISCO PREMIUM – 16OZ.
STORE A

The Marketing Fact Book.

DISPLAY
DISP & FEAT
NO PROMO

WEEKLY PRICE

promotional periods. It is normally the standard of comparison for the incremental sales generated by a promotion, or the level of business that should be increased if promotion were to have any long-term effect.

Saltine crackers provide a good product category to examine. In Figures 3-19 through 3-22 three competitive brands, along with private brands and generic brands, are shown for Store A. Keebler had two reasonably successful promotions in June and February, but the normal base business sales line remains almost perfectly horizontal. Nabisco had a relatively successful promotion in January, and several others that appear to have been somewhat less successful. The base business line again appears to be relatively flat, even though it fluctuates throughout the chart. Sunshine Krispy had one very successful promotion in October, yet the fundamental base business did not change. The conclusion drawn is that promotion has very little, if any, impact on base business.

If a brand reduces its promotional effort, clearly the sales volume will decrease, moving back to the base level of business. If a brand increases the promotional effort, the sales volume during the promotional period will increase. It is important to remember that the sales volume changes do not necessarily mean that the profit will change as well. A reduction in promotional effort will result in sales volume decrease, but may result in an increase

Figure 3-21

SUNSHINE KRISPY SALTINES
STORE A

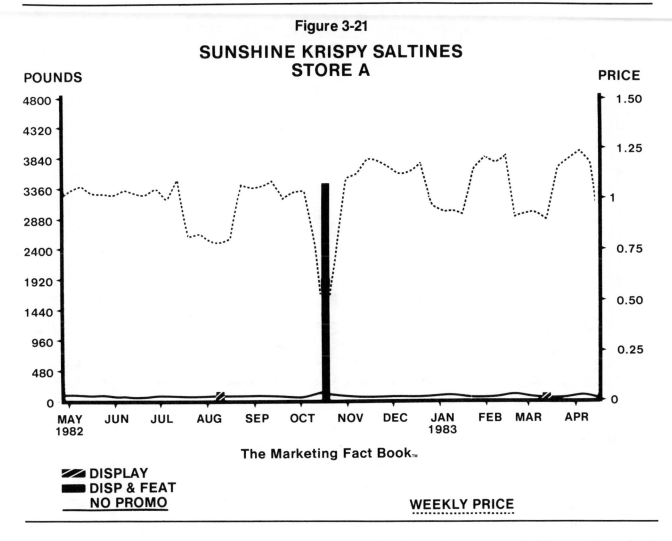

The Marketing Fact Book™

DISPLAY
DISP & FEAT
NO PROMO

WEEKLY PRICE

in profits because the margin is higher. Hence, a careful financial analysis should be performed for every sales promotion program to assess its profitability. Relying entirely on sales volume could be very misleading.

Case: Saltine Crackers

Saltine crackers provide an interesting case history to examine the impact of sales promotion. Saltines are sold primarily through food stores and are frequently promoted by both the manufacturer and the retailer. This case is based upon 80 weeks of scanner sales history in one city. Please answer all of the questions at the end of the case.

Background Saltine crackers are purchased by over 80 percent of all households. On the average, the time between purchases is around 80 days. Sales promotion, including features, displays, and price reductions are extremely important in this category, with around 50 percent of annual category sales moving with some sort of sales promotion. Shelf price reductions, when they are used, average about 25 percent.

The major competitors in this category are:

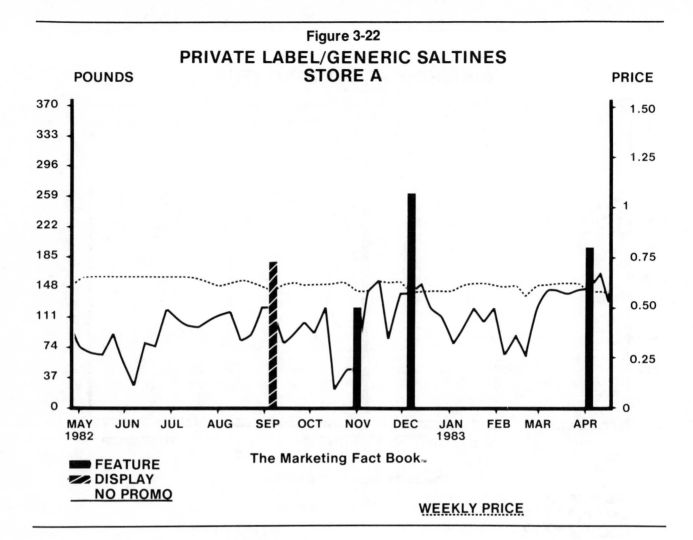

Figure 3-22
PRIVATE LABEL/GENERIC SALTINES
STORE A

POUNDS

PRICE

■ FEATURE
▨ DISPLAY
__ NO PROMO

The Marketing Fact Book™

WEEKLY PRICE

Brands	Share
Nabisco Premium	44.1
Keebler Zesta	20.0
Sunshine Krispy	10.1
Other Branded	4.4
Private Label	16.3
Generic	5.1

The data for this case were collected from grocery store scanner installations in one market area and consist of:
1. Weekly store sales by brand
2. Predominant price charged by brand by store
3. Occurrence of promotional activity by brand by store

The data have been summarized across all stores in the market on a weekly basis for a total of 80 weeks. Further summarization has been made in several different tables. Table 3-1 is a summary of 10 eight-week periods. Table 3-2 is a summary of four-week periods. Table 3-3 is the week-by-week summary.

At the weekly level, Table 3-4 shows the data on the amount of volume moved by various promotions at various prices. However, since the stores in the market are of varying sizes, direct evaluation of promotion effects is difficult. Table 3-5 is the result of normalizing the sales effects to reflect the relative store sizes in which the sales occur. Normalizing is a statistical process which in effect adjusts for the size of the store. Typical methods for store scanner data are: (1) brand volume per $1,000.00 total all commodity volume spending, and (2) brand volume per 1,000 register checkouts.

During the time of data collection, some extremely "hot" promotional activity occurred as the result of a Keebler promotional program. There were decisions by some retailers to use Zesta crackers as a loss-leader, in addition to manufacturer promotions and combinations of both. These activities resulted in substantial variations in price, volume, and share of Zesta.

Table 3-1
CITY SALES OF KEEBLER ZESTA CRACKERS BY 8-WEEK PERIODS
PRICE IS VOLUME WEIGHTED AVERAGE

BI-MO	ZESTA VOLUME	ZESTA PRICE	ZESTA SHARE
1	8478	0.721	17.1
2	20199	0.216	39.5
3	10695	0.903	25.4
4	5586	0.822	9.0
5	3921	1.049	8.5
6	17091	0.652	24.3
7	7197	0.731	13.3
8	4953	0.995	11.1
9	3555	1.071	9.7
10	6384	0.957	12.9

Table 3-2
CITY SALES OF KEEBLER ZESTA CRACKERS BY 4-WEEK PERIODS
PRICE IS VOLUME WEIGHTED AVERAGE

MONTH	ZESTA VOLUME	ZESTA PRICE	ZESTA SHARE
1	2643	0.795	10.0
2	5835	0.688	25.4
3	17835	0.127	52.2
4	2364	0.888	13.9
5	1524	0.985	9.0
6	9171	0.889	36.3
7	2145	0.907	7.8
8	3441	0.769	10.0
9	2067	1.012	8.5
10	1854	1.090	8.4
11	1494	1.116	4.2
12	15597	0.608	44.6
13	2433	1.011	8.6
14	4764	0.589	18.5
15	2361	0.989	10.1
16	2592	1.000	12.3
17	2052	1.040	11.0
18	1503	1.114	8.4
19	3897	0.946	18.3
20	2487	0.974	8.8

Table 3-3
CITY SALES OF KEEBLER ZESTA CRACKERS BY WEEK
PRICE IS VOLUME WEIGHTED AVERAGE

WEEK	ZESTA VOLUME	ZESTA DOLLARS	CATEGORY VOLUME	CATEGORY DOLLARS	ZESTA PRICE	ZESTA SHARE	COMPETITIVE VOLUME
1	306	250.98	5984.4	4356.03	0.820	5.1	5678.4
2	564	440.52	8706.9	7496.10	0.781	6.5	8142.9
3	873	694.35	6201.9	4893.48	0.795	14.1	5328.9
4	900	715.50	5657.6	4447.38	0.795	15.9	4757.6
5	4404	2772.54	7673.8	5453.01	0.630	57.4	3269.8
6	456	388.44	5027.3	4196.04	0.852	9.1	4571.3
7	444	395.46	5570.4	4687.35	0.891	8.0	5126.4
8	531	459.09	4737.4	3984.81	0.865	11.2	4206.4
9	483	441.27	4661.4	3917.40	0.914	10.4	4178.4
10	615	548.55	4803.9	4381.80	0.892	12.8	4188.9
11	624	571.68	5038.9	4632.21	0.916	12.4	4414.9
12	16113	705.58	19633.5	3982.51	0.044	82.1	3520.5
13	1056	811.14	4476.2	3967.17	0.768	23.6	3420.2
14	381	375.45	3863.1	3599.01	0.985	9.9	3482.1
15	534	526.50	5014.3	4677.78	0.986	10.6	4480.3
16	393	387.21	3675.9	3387.57	0.985	10.7	3282.9
17	390	384.36	3642.2	3350.64	0.986	10.7	3252.2
18	405	398.67	3743.4	3441.75	0.984	10.8	3338.4
19	381	375.09	4755.2	4184.64	0.984	8.0	4374.2
20	348	342.90	4733.4	4248.57	0.985	7.4	4385.4
21	378	372.06	3862.3	3448.92	0.984	9.8	3484.3
22	5319	5129.31	8352.9	7839.45	0.964	63.7	3033.9
23	2280	1691.40	7086.4	5311.35	0.742	32.2	4806.4
24	1194	962.76	5931.9	4878.36	0.806	20.1	4737.9
25	1020	837.00	5708.3	4666.20	0.821	17.9	4688.3
26	342	336.96	7780.9	5849.10	0.985	4.4	7438.9
27	363	357.57	6714.9	5259.72	0.985	5.4	6351.9
28	420	413.76	7352.3	5533.23	0.985	5.7	6932.3
29	528	520.98	7516.1	5661.03	0.987	7.0	6988.1
30	942	676.38	6416.8	5461.17	0.718	14.7	5474.8
31	957	711.33	15599.3	7578.66	0.743	6.1	14642.3
32	1014	738.96	4937.4	4294.65	0.729	20.5	3923.4
33	1059	990.51	5664.6	5213.88	0.935	18.7	4605.6
34	351	385.92	9045.9	7302.30	1.099	3.9	8694.9
35	384	418.56	5435.6	4932.57	1.090	7.1	5051.6
36	273	297.57	4088.1	3658.98	1.090	6.7	3815.1
37	411	447.99	6305.6	5540.01	1.090	6.5	5894.6
38	498	542.82	5643.0	5103.30	1.090	8.8	5145.0
39	459	500.31	5555.4	5150.49	1.090	8.3	5096.4
40	486	529.74	4485.2	4285.50	1.090	10.8	3999.2

Table 3-3 (CONTINUED)

WEEK	ZESTA VOLUME	ZESTA DOLLARS	CATEGORY VOLUME	CATEGORY DOLLARS	ZESTA PRICE	ZESTA SHARE	COMPETITIVE VOLUME
41	378	422.82	4665.4	4191.87	1.119	8.1	4287.4
42	345	384.15	14288.3	9780.39	1.113	2.4	13943.3
43	420	468.60	9073.3	7483.91	1.116	4.6	8653.3
44	351	392.31	7355.3	6306.99	1.118	4.8	7004.3
45	378	423.18	6703.5	5914.62	1.120	5.6	6325.5
46	4122	3084.90	8672.3	7699.32	0.748	47.5	4550.3
47	9108	4466.31	13165.5	8694.36	0.490	69.2	4057.5
48	1989	1501.48	6393.0	5881.21	0.755	31.1	4404.0
49	1164	1043.04	5635.7	5333.49	0.896	20.7	4471.7
50	414	461.70	7823.6	6981.42	1.115	5.3	7409.6
51	432	483.12	8083.3	6351.69	1.118	5.3	7651.3
52	423	471.51	6796.1	5268.36	1.115	6.2	6373.1
53	537	598.65	6868.3	6009.57	1.115	7.8	6331.3
54	1821	870.69	6487.1	5257.86	0.478	28.1	4666.1
55	1260	324.24	6245.3	4823.36	0.257	20.2	4985.3
56	1146	1011.54	6126.4	5556.51	0.883	18.7	4980.4
57	1152	1012.89	5042.8	4865.88	0.879	22.8	3890.8
58	501	552.90	6459.6	5008.51	1.104	7.8	5958.6
59	390	424.05	6261.2	4776.09	1.087	6.2	5871.2
60	318	344.61	5635.7	4779.48	1.084	5.6	5317.7
61	405	450.15	6605.1	5603.70	1.111	6.1	6200.1
62	420	466.08	4662.8	4557.63	1.110	9.0	4242.8
63	483	536.37	4700.4	4655.28	1.110	10.3	4217.4
64	1284	1139.82	5099.4	4827.15	0.888	25.2	3815.4
65	657	583.56	6480.8	5043.96	0.888	10.1	5823.8
66	432	478.80	3636.8	3583.56	1.108	11.9	3204.8
67	546	608.10	4651.5	4701.06	1.114	11.7	4105.5
68	417	463.53	3964.5	3989.73	1.112	10.5	3547.5
69	312	348.36	4605.8	4049.51	1.117	6.8	4293.8
70	330	368.16	4119.2	4004.35	1.116	8.0	3789.1
71	399	443.55	4455.9	4348.20	1.112	9.0	4056.9
72	462	514.02	4813.7	4803.63	1.113	9.6	4351.7
73	411	457.53	5097.8	4907.46	1.113	8.1	4686.8
74	897	823.14	5379.8	5089.38	0.918	16.7	4482.8
75	1509	1378.32	5385.2	5191.83	0.913	28.0	3876.2
76	1080	1027.08	5473.5	5380.14	0.951	19.7	4393.5
77	921	887.73	4902.6	4851.90	0.964	18.8	3981.6
78	513	507.60	11519.6	8305.66	0.989	4.5	11006.6
79	567	549.54	5396.3	4661.40	0.969	10.5	4829.3
80	486	478.68	6406.3	5538.69	0.985	7.6	5920.3

Table 3-4
CITY SALES OF KEEBLER ZESTA CRACKERS BY WEEK
PRICE IS VOLUME WEIGHTED AVERAGE
SALES BY PROMOTIONAL TYPE

WEEK	VOLUME WITH NO PROMOTION	PRICE WITH NO PROMOTION	VOL. W/ DISPLAY ONLY	PRICE W/ DISPLAY ONLY	VOL. W/ FEATURE ONLY	PRICE W/ FEATURE ONLY	VOL. W/ FEAT. & DISPLAY	PRICE W/ FEAT. & DISPLAY
1	306	0.82	0	.	0	.	0	.
2	564	0.78	0	.	0	.	0	.
3	477	0.75	396	0.85	0	.	0	.
4	420	0.75	480	0.84	0	.	0	.
5	222	0.69	0	.	0	.	4182	0.63
6	399	0.83	57	0.99	0	.	0	.
7	375	0.87	69	0.99	0	.	0	.
8	531	0.87	0	.	0	.	0	.
9	405	0.90	78	0.99	0	.	0	.
10	486	0.87	129	0.99	0	.	0	.
11	537	0.90	87	0.99	0	.	0	.
12	486	0.79	102	0.85	0	.	15525	0.02
13	384	0.75	0	.	0	.	672	0.78
14	381	0.99	0	.	0	.	0	.
15	534	0.99	0	.	0	.	0	.
16	393	0.99	0	.	0	.	0	.
17	390	0.99	0	.	0	.	0	.
18	405	0.98	0	.	0	.	0	.
19	381	0.98	0	.	0	.	0	.
20	348	0.99	0	.	0	.	0	.
21	378	0.98	0	.	0	.	0	.
22	201	0.69	0	.	0	.	5118	0.98
23	0	.	702	0.86	1578	0.69	0	.
24	819	0.86	375	0.69	0	.	0	.
25	366	0.74	654	0.86	0	.	0	.
26	252	0.98	90	0.99	0	.	0	.
27	285	0.98	78	0.99	0	.	0	.
28	327	0.98	93	0.99	0	.	0	.
29	309	0.98	219	0.99	0	.	0	.
30	588	0.74	354	0.69	0	.	0	.
31	450	0.73	507	0.75	0	.	0	.
32	333	0.69	288	0.69	195	0.79	198	0.79
33	555	0.87	504	1.01	0	.	0	.
34	303	1.10	48	1.12	0	.	0	.
35	384	1.09	0	.	0	.	0	.
36	273	1.09	0	.	0	.	0	.
37	411	1.09	0	.	0	.	0	.
38	498	1.09	0	.	0	.	0	.
39	459	1.09	0	.	0	.	0	.
40	486	1.09	0	.	0	.	0	.

Table 3-4 (CONTINUED)

WEEK	VOLUME WITH NO PROMOTION	PRICE WITH NO PROMOTION	VOL. W/ DISPLAY ONLY	PRICE W/ DISPLAY ONLY	VOL. W/ FEATURE ONLY	PRICE W/ FEATURE ONLY	VOL. W/ FEAT. & DISPLAY	PRICE W/ FEAT. & DISPLAY
41	378	1.12	0	.	0	.	0	.
42	345	1.11	0	.	0	.	0	.
43	420	1.12	0	.	0	.	0	.
44	351	1.12	0	.	0	.	0	.
45	378	1.12	0	.	0	.	0	.
46	132	0.89	0	.	0	.	3990	0.74
47	0	.	2409	0.74	0	.	6699	0.40
48	246	0.69	1743	0.76	0	.	0	.
49	459	0.91	705	0.89	0	.	0	.
50	111	1.12	303	1.11	0	.	0	.
51	153	1.12	279	1.12	0	.	0	.
52	240	1.11	183	1.13	0	.	0	.
53	321	1.10	216	1.13	0	.	0	.
54	267	0.87	153	0.98	0	.	1401	0.35
55	369	0.87	891	0.01	0	.	0	.
56	504	0.87	642	0.90	0	.	0	.
57	315	0.81	672	0.89	60	0.98	105	0.98
58	462	1.10	39	1.14	0	.	0	.
59	390	1.09	0	.	0	.	0	.
60	318	1.08	0	.	0	.	0	.
61	405	1.11	0	.	0	.	0	.
62	420	1.11	0	.	0	.	0	.
63	483	1.11	0	.	0	.	0	.
64	501	0.90	783	0.88	0	.	0	.
65	378	0.87	279	0.92	0	.	0	.
66	246	1.10	186	1.12	0	.	0	.
67	315	1.11	231	1.12	0	.	0	.
68	417	1.11	0	.	0	.	0	.
69	312	1.12	0	.	0	.	0	.
70	330	1.12	0	.	0	.	0	.
71	399	1.11	0	.	0	.	0	.
72	462	1.11	0	.	0	.	0	.
73	411	1.11	0	.	0	.	0	.
74	495	0.95	402	0.88	0	.	0	.
75	117	0.99	288	0.99	585	0.89	519	0.88
76	156	0.98	924	0.95	0	.	0	.
77	222	0.91	699	0.98	0	.	0	.
78	471	0.98	42	1.07	0	.	0	.
79	399	0.95	168	1.02	0	.	0	.
80	486	0.99	0	.	0	.	0	.

Table 3-5
CITY SALES OF KEEBLER ZESTA CRACKERS BY WEEK
PRICE IS VOLUME WEIGHTED AVERAGE
NORMALIZED VOLUME SALES BY PROMOTIONAL TYPE

WEEK	NORM. VOL. NO PROMOTION	PRICE WITH NO PROMOTION	NORM. VOL. DISPLAY ONLY	PRICE W/ DISPLAY ONLY	NORM. VOL. FEATURE ONLY	PRICE W/ FEATURE ONLY	NORM. VOL. FEAT. & DISPLAY	PRICE W/ FEAT. & DISPLAY
1	0.21	0.82	0.00	.	0.00	.	0.00	.
2	0.38	0.78	0.00	.	0.00	.	0.00	.
3	0.45	0.75	0.66	0.85	0.00	.	0.00	.
4	0.50	0.75	0.63	0.84	0.00	.	0.00	.
5	0.60	0.69	0.00	.	0.00	.	3.94	0.63
6	0.33	0.83	0.32	0.99	0.00	.	0.00	.
7	0.24	0.87	0.36	0.99	0.00	.	0.00	.
8	0.34	0.87	0.00	.	0.00	.	0.00	.
9	0.30	0.90	0.34	0.99	0.00	.	0.00	.
10	0.36	0.87	0.50	0.99	0.00	.	0.00	.
11	0.41	0.90	0.41	0.99	0.00	.	0.00	.
12	0.50	0.79	0.45	0.85	0.00	.	3.95	0.02
13	0.38	0.75	0.00	.	0.00	.	1.14	0.78
14	0.25	0.99	0.00	.	0.00	.	0.00	.
15	0.26	0.99	0.00	.	0.00	.	0.00	.
16	0.25	0.98	0.00	.	0.00	.	0.00	.
17	0.25	0.99	0.00	.	0.00	.	0.00	.
18	0.27	0.98	0.00	.	0.00	.	0.00	.
19	0.25	0.98	0.00	.	0.00	.	0.00	.
20	0.21	0.99	0.00	.	0.00	.	0.00	.
21	0.27	0.98	0.00	.	0.00	.	0.00	.
22	0.57	0.69	0.00	.	0.00	.	4.79	0.98
23	0.00	.	0.64	0.86	3.77	0.69	0.00	.
24	0.65	0.86	0.98	0.69	0.00	.	0.00	.
25	0.55	0.74	0.80	0.86	0.00	.	0.00	.
26	0.21	0.98	0.28	0.99	0.00	.	0.00	.
27	0.23	0.98	0.26	0.99	0.00	.	0.00	.
28	0.26	0.98	0.29	0.99	0.00	.	0.00	.
29	0.24	0.98	0.67	0.99	0.00	.	0.00	.
30	0.48	0.74	1.15	0.69	0.00	.	0.00	.
31	0.45	0.73	0.95	0.75	0.00	.	0.00	.
32	0.55	0.69	0.93	0.69	0.96	0.79	0.55	0.79
33	0.52	0.87	0.88	1.01	0.00	.	0.00	.
34	0.22	1.10	0.36	1.12	0.00	.	0.00	.
35	0.25	1.09	0.00	.	0.00	.	0.00	.
36	0.19	1.09	0.00	.	0.00	.	0.00	.
37	0.25	1.09	0.00	.	0.00	.	0.00	.
38	0.29	1.09	0.00	.	0.00	.	0.00	.
39	0.26	1.09	0.00	.	0.00	.	0.00	.
40	0.29	1.09	0.00	.	0.00	.	0.00	.

Table 3-5 (CONTINUED)

WEEK	NORM. VOL. NO PROMOTION	PRICE WITH NO PROMOTION	NORM. VOL. DISPLAY ONLY	PRICE W/ DISPLAY ONLY	NORM. VOL. FEATURE ONLY	PRICE W/ FEATURE ONLY	NORM. VOL. FEAT. & DISPLAY	PRICE W/ FEAT. & DISPLAY
41	0.26	1.12	0.00	.	0.00	.	0.00	.
42	0.20	1.11	0.00	.	0.00	.	0.00	.
43	0.25	1.12	0.00	.	0.00	.	0.00	.
44	0.21	1.12	0.00	.	0.00	.	0.00	.
45	0.24	1.12	0.00	.	0.00	.	0.00	.
46	0.37	0.89	0.00	.	0.00	.	2.98	0.74
47	0.00	.	1.92	0.74	0.00	.	18.61	0.40
48	2.44	0.69	1.16	0.76	0.00	.	0.00	.
49	0.51	0.91	1.14	0.89	0.00	.	0.00	.
50	0.18	1.12	0.28	1.11	0.00	.	0.00	.
51	0.23	1.12	0.29	1.12	0.00	.	0.00	.
52	0.22	1.11	0.32	1.13	0.00	.	0.00	.
53	0.30	1.10	0.38	1.13	0.00	.	0.00	.
54	0.34	0.87	0.65	0.98	0.00	.	2.05	0.35
55	0.49	0.87	1.12	0.01	0.00	.	0.00	.
56	0.56	0.87	0.87	0.90	0.00	.	0.00	.
57	0.70	0.81	1.85	0.89	0.15	0.98	0.48	0.98
58	0.33	1.10	0.26	1.14	0.00	.	0.00	.
59	0.23	1.10	0.00	.	0.00	.	0.00	.
60	0.19	1.08	0.00	.	0.00	.	0.00	.
61	0.25	1.11	0.00	.	0.00	.	0.00	.
62	0.23	1.11	0.00	.	0.00	.	0.00	.
63	0.31	1.11	0.00	.	0.00	.	0.00	.
64	0.49	0.90	1.17	0.88	0.00	.	0.00	.
65	0.33	0.87	0.48	0.92	0.00	.	0.00	.
66	0.24	1.10	0.30	1.12	0.00	.	0.00	.
67	0.26	1.11	0.31	1.12	0.00	.	0.00	.
68	0.26	1.11	0.00	.	0.00	.	0.00	.
69	0.19	1.12	0.00	.	0.00	.	0.00	.
70	0.20	1.12	0.00	.	0.00	.	0.00	.
71	0.24	1.11	0.00	.	0.00	.	0.00	.
72	0.26	1.11	0.00	.	0.00	.	0.00	.
73	0.23	1.11	0.00	.	0.00	.	0.00	.
74	0.40	0.95	1.00	0.88	0.00	.	0.00	.
75	0.43	0.99	0.82	0.99	1.55	0.89	0.79	0.88
76	0.51	0.98	0.55	0.95	0.00	.	0.00	.
77	0.46	0.91	0.63	0.98	0.00	.	0.00	.
78	0.31	0.98	0.27	1.07	0.00	.	0.00	.
79	0.32	0.95	0.48	1.02	0.00	.	0.00	.
80	0.30	0.99	0.00	.	0.00	.	0.00	.

Question 1   Using Table 3-1, plot Zesta's bi-monthly volume versus bi-monthly price. Plot Zesta's bi-monthly share versus bi-monthly price. Given that Zesta's normal shelf price is around 99¢ per pound during non-promotional conditions, what do these plots suggest would be the impact on Zesta's volume and share if the price were raised to $1.09 per pound?

Question 2   Using Table 3-2, plot Zesta's monthly volume versus Zesta's monthly price, and plot Zesta's monthly share versus Zesta's monthly price. Given that Zesta's normal shelf price is around 99¢ per pound during non-promotional conditions, what do these plots suggest would be the impact on Zesta's volume and share if the price were raised to $1.09 per pound?

Question 3   Using Table 3, estimate the impact of raising the price from 99¢ to $1.09 per pound on Zesta's volume and share. Plot Zesta's city volume versus price and Zesta's city share versus price.

Question 4   According to Table 3-3, Weeks 5, 12, 22, 23, 46, and 47 are highly important sales weeks for Zesta. Weeks 31, 42, and 78 are important sales weeks for the competition. If data on promotional activity are not known, its presence is usually inferred by abnormally high sales of the brand or category, a cut in price, or both. Reviewing these weeks, and nearby weeks, discuss the impacts on Zesta and its competitors on:
1. Total category volume
2. Total category dollar spending
3. Each other's volume (Zesta's and competitors')
4. Sales in the weeks following high volume movement

Question 5   Table 3-4 shows overall promotional activity. Sales during Week 12 are at an average price near zero. This typically arises out of a retail promotion of the type: "Free box of Zesta saltines given with total purchases of $10.00 or more." Table 3-5 shows sales levels adjusted for the percentage of stores in each class, and for their relative sizes. Discuss any difficulties you see in assessing the impact of the Week 12 promotion on:
1. Incremental volume to Zesta
2. Promotional volume borrowed from future sales

Question 6   Using Table 3-5, plot only the non-promoted sales versus the non-promoted price. Discuss the probable percent impact on Zesta sales from a 10 percent increase or decrease in price. How does this change compare with the impact of trade dealing? (Hint: Use Table 3, Weeks 29 to 80, to assess the contribution of trade dealing to total Zesta volume.)

Question 7   Using Table 3-5, plot the relation between sales on display only, and display only price. What similarities and differences in sales levels and response to price do you see in comparing the display only response to the non-promotional response?

4 *Manufacturer Controlled Strategies*

❈❈❈❈❈❈❈❈❈❈❈❈❈❈❈❈❈❈❈❈❈❈❈❈❈❈❈❈❈❈❈❈❈❈

Sales promotion programs can come from two sources, the manufacturer and the retailer. Promotion programs that originate from the retailer are considered in the next chapter. Promotion programs that originate from the manufacturer are always aimed at the final consumer, although the approach may be either indirect or direct. An indirect manufacturer controlled promotion strategy is aimed at the trade, or wholesalers and retailers, with the hope that as a result, they will influence the final consumer through their selling efforts. A direct manufacturer controlled promotion program is aimed directly at the final consumer.

Promotion to the Consumer

A manufacturer has perhaps the widest range of choices in the type of promotion to use when aiming directly at the final consumer. A manufacturer may use virtually any of the price promotions, including coupons, price-offs, rebates, and bonus packs. In addition, a manufacturer may use any of the interest promotions, such as premiums, contests, and sweepstakes. The only form of sales promotion that the manufacturer can't use directly to the consumer is the trade allowance.

Consumer promotions can be difficult to manage for several reasons. The first problem is getting the promotion distributed to the consumer. As discussed before, the manufacturer has a wide variety of choices, including paid mass media delivery, such as newspaper free standing inserts, in-store displays with tear-off pads, or an on- or in-package delivery.

Each method has its own special problems. Media delivery has the problems of relatively high cost and waste circulation. In-store displays need the cooperation of the retailer, which may require a supporting trade promotion. On- or in-package delivery may not reach non-purchasers or purchasers of other brands. Delivery of the promotion to the consumer is usually a major component of the cost of the promotional effort.

A second problem involves redemption or fulfillment. A price-off pack avoids this problem, but is very expensive because the special price is given to all purchasers of the product, including those who would have purchased the product without the benefit of the promotion. Redeeming coupons involves not only the cost of the face value of the coupon, but also the cost of the handling of the coupon. Redemption rate can also be an important issue, especially if it is much higher than expected. If a free-in-the-mail or self-liquidating premium is used, then fulfillment, or getting the premium delivered to the consumer, is an important issue. The same is true for both contests and sweepstakes.

A third problem is high cost. A manufacturer promoting directly to the consumer most likely will pay the highest delivery rates. A retailer enjoys the lower local newspaper media rate, whereas a manufacturer would most likely have to pay the higher national rate. This is because a direct consumer promotion from a manufacturer does not have the benefit of any cost sharing with retailers. One exception is manufacturer coupons, which may be combined with local retailer double or triple coupon value promotions.

Consumer promotions do have a major advantage despite their difficulties in administration. For example, the manufacturer has complete control over the timing and method of promotion, rather than depending on the whim of the retailer. The manufacturer can be certain of the form and method of promotion, as well as the critical issue of timing. In essence, the manufacturer in direct promotion does not relinquish any control of the promotional program, while it may with an indirect promotional program.

Promotion to the Trade

Indirect promotions are designed to influence wholesalers and retailers, who in turn will influence the final consumer. The first problem with promotion to the trade is that the linkage just described works with different levels of efficiency. Sometimes the retailer decides to take full advantage of a trade promotion offered by a manufacturer and to add considerably more to it, making the indirect trade promotion far more effective than an equivalent direct consumer promotion. On the other hand, sometimes a retailer ignores the trade promotion altogether and makes no changes in the pricing, display, or store advertising of the product. Other times the retailer will do something in between these two extremes.

Probably the most pervasive form of trade promotion is the trade allowance, which is simply a short-term reduction in the selling price to the trade. Presumably this incentive will induce the trade to promote the particular product over competing products, or perhaps even over other product categories. Trade promotion may also include coupons, contests, and other things as discussed before.

Perhaps more important than implementing a temporary reduction in price to the final consumer is the use of trade promotion to gain the cooperation of the retailer in support of other promotional and marketing programs. Getting a retailer to use in-store displays, ad features, or to provide valuable shelf space may be critically important to the success of a marketing program and may be only accomplished through the use of effective trade promotion.

The major disadvantage of trade promotion from the perspective of the manufacturer is the loss of managerial control. The retailer may or may not take advantage of the promotion, and may not pass through to the consumer the full benefits of the promotion as well. While it might seem a simple solution to establish stringent criteria for the retailer's use of the promotion, such criteria are often difficult to enforce. This is especially true of large retailers who represent substantial sales volume and are in an extremely competitive environment.

Despite any problems, trade promotions are a necessary part of business for most manufacturers. In fact, it is quite difficult for a manufacturer to implement any marketing strategy without a trade promotion component.

Distribution Channel Management

Ideally the manufacturer would like to be the dominant force in the distribution channel, which includes the manufacturer, wholesalers, and retailers. The manufacturer should be able to maximize profitability with strong brands that are demanded by consumers, forcing the trade to comply with the strategies of the manufacturer in order to have products to sell. Unfortunately, from the perspective of the manufacturer, this type of channel control rarely exists.

Trade promotion is one tool the manufacturer now has to gain the cooperation of the trade, but it may be diminishing in its effectiveness. As retailers increase in their concentration, or become part of larger chains, their marketplace power increases. It is a common prediction that the trend toward increased retail concentration will continue in the future. This may mean that the retailer, not the manufacturer, will be the dominant force in the distribution channel. Thus the giant retail chain, with its access to the final consumer, may well be in a position to dictate its marketing strategy to the manufacturer. Certainly the relative strength of the retail chain contributes to the importance of trade promotion. In 1986, the nine largest chains were estimated to control about 30 percent of all retail grocery sales.

One result of the increasing retail concentration is a substantially more sophisticated retailer. This is especially apparent in food retailing. The larger chains are beginning to view their shelf space on a profit center basis and are employing increasingly sophisticated models in its allocation. Obviously it is necessary for the manufacturers to increase their sophistication to remain competitive.

Brand Family Management

Most manufacturers have both multiple lines within a single brand and multiple brands. The obvious consideration in the promotion of any single brand or line is the impact that its promotion may have on other lines and brands. The manufacturer needs to decide how to allocate promotional dollars most efficiently across both brands and lines to maximize profit.

The critical question is how much of the benefit of the promotion of one brand or of one line benefits others. Most of the evidence suggests that, while there might be some benefit, it is probably minimal. The seeming inability of sales promotion of established brands to produce increased long-term sales volume after a promotion and the differential effects of package size suggest sales promotion would have a minimal sales impact on other brands in the family. However, there might be some negative impact on related brands and lines if one is so heavily promoted that the brand image is damaged. How much this might impact related brands and other lines is not clearly understood, but there may well be some effect. The manager should certainly examine the profitability of each member of the entire brand family to assess this potential impact.

Competitive Activity

An interesting finding from the examination of scanner data is that the direct effects on competition from a single promotional effort are minimal. In other words, the promotional program of one brand at one point in time does not appear to have much impact on the level of business of competing brands. It is also true that when there are competing promotions within the same product category, there is some tendency to reduce the impact of both in terms of incremental business.

In the short term at least, sales promotion does not seem to have much impact on the base level of business, but it certainly has considerable impact on incremental business, and hence on overall market share. If one brand does not promote, and another promotes heavily, the heavily promoted brand should enjoy a higher share. There is, then, pressure to meet competitive promotional levels to maintain market share. However, all too often, short-term promotional volume is purchased at the expense of overall brand profitability.

A brand must maintain the promotional levels established by the competing brands within a product category in order to maintain the status quo, and must balance share and profitability considerations. This means that manufacturers must continuously monitor competing promotions to be certain that the competitive edge is not lost.

Manufacturer Decisions

There are a number of critical decisions that a manufacturer must make each time a promotional program is being considered. The decisions for the most part cross the boundaries of both consumer and trade promotions. These decisions are summarized in the following six categories.

Feature Promotion

Probably the first decision is whether or not to include the promotion in the advertising program. A manufacturer may want to include the promotion in its national advertising plans. For example, coupons might be included in magazine advertisements. Other promotions, such as contests or sweepstakes, premiums, or special packages also might be components of the national advertising program.

The manufacturer may also attempt to influence the retailer to feature a promotion in its advertising through cooperative advertising offers. Making available the appropriate advertising copy and a sufficiently attractive cooperative agreement would certainly increase the likelihood that the retailer would feature the promotion. The evidence clearly demonstrates that featuring a promotion in supporting advertising greatly enhances its impact.

Generally, the manufacturer can manipulate the ratios in a co-operative advertising program, including both the proportion of the advertising expense it is willing to reimburse the retailer, and the maximum proportion of sales it is willing to reimburse. For example, a manufacturer may reimburse up to 50 percent of the cost of the advertising space or time purchased by the retailer up to a maximum of 3 percent of the gross purchases the retailer makes from the manufacturer during some specified period of time. Increasing the proportion of the advertising expense that the manufacturer will reimburse to the retailer or increasing the maximum percentage of sales should be part of the consideration of the profitability analysis of the promotion.

Displays

Like advertising, the use of in-store displays clearly enhances the impact of a promotion. Displays alone generate more sales, but not nearly as much as displays with a special price. So in general, a display, if it can be used, will substantially improve sales. For most product categories, an in-store display without feature advertising generates a higher level of sales than an advertising feature without an in-store display at the same price.

A manufacturer may prepare and distribute display materials to the retailer. This can represent a substantial expense depending on the complexity and the nature of the display. A hidden cost in the use of displays is the additional promotional support needed to get the retailer to use the display.

Most retailers receive many more displays or display offers than they can possibly use. Hence, it is also necessary to offer trade price promotion support to gain the necessary cooperation. Locations such as the most desirable high traffic areas within the store are especially in demand. Some cases, like the special positions such as front aisle ends, require a direct payment to the retailer. Again, all of the costs should be included in a profitability analysis against the increased sales volume the display is expected to generate.

Additional Allowances for the Retailer

How much of a trade allowance to provide the retailer is always an important consideration. Presumably the greater the allowance, the greater the likelihood of obtaining retailer cooperation. Additional allowances may also increase the chance that the retailer will provide additional effort in the promotion. Again, based upon past experience, the increase in trade allowance should be carefully evaluated in terms of potential profitability.

Raise Shelf Price

Another possible strategy is to raise shelf price. If the brand is strong, an announced higher shelf price may have the same effect as an increased trade allowance as it makes the current price lower than the future price. This decision would depend upon the relative position of the brand and competitive conditions within the product category. A key consideration is assessing probable competitive reaction.

Promotion Duration

The length of time the promotion should be in effect is another critical manufacturer decision. On the one hand the manufacturer wants to be certain that consumers have enough time to respond, and on the other hand the promotion should not last so long that it becomes accepted as the normal selling condition. An important consideration would be the normal purchase cycle, or average length of time between purchases. Retailers are also likely to cooperate only for limited periods of time.

The type of promotion is also important. Contests and sweepstakes, for example, should probably last longer than the purchase cycle for most grocery store products. The same is true for manufacturer distributed coupons because the consumer needs time to take advantage of the offer during the normal purchase cycle. As a practical matter, it is difficult to obtain advertising features or in-store displays for periods of time much longer than a week, except in highly seasonal categories.

Package Size

Selecting the proper package size to promote is critical in the success of a promotional program. It is important to select the most appropriate package size for the target market. As discussed before, different geographic markets, even different demographic segments, purchase different package sizes. The decision of which package size or sizes to promote should be carefully considered in terms of the marketing objectives.

Introducing New Products

A special marketing problem is the introduction of new products. A new product has two unique problems when compared to established products—no shelf space and no consumer experience. Sales promotion can be used to help remedy both problems.

Projecting Sales from Test Markets

New products are an especially difficult problem for most manufacturers. The overwhelming majority of new products do not succeed in the marketplace; thus there is a need to be able to distinguish the winning products from the others. Typically a method used to experiment with new products is the test market. A test market is simply a representative single market area that allows the performance of a new product to be evaluated with a minimum of investment in the product itself and associated marketing expenses.

Measuring the results from the test market and controlling the various marketing variables that influence the success or failure of the product are traditional problems with test markets. For example, an excellent product may appear to fail because competitive advertising and promotion overwhelm it.

A solution to some of these problems has been the availability of the electronic test market complete with scanner panels and targetable television. The use of these sophisticated systems has greatly improved the ability to discriminate between successful and unsuccessful products. The electronic test markets have also reduced the time necessary to make the judgment from the test. Perhaps one shortcoming of these test facilities is the inability to test trade reaction to the new product. The access through the trade to the consumer is forced, with the focus of the test on consumer reaction to the product.

Product categories that are not sold through grocery or drug outlets may not be easily tested using electronic test markets. However, the testing capabilities are being expanded to include other types of outlets, including general merchandise stores. The selection and design of test market experiments is itself a complex subject, which is made considerably more complex when the models and procedures for projecting sales from them are also included. Whenever possible, the same high quality data should be employed to evaluate new products as that used to evaluate sales promotion programs.

Obtaining Distribution

Getting access to valuable shelf space for any product, new or established, is a difficult task. Convincing retailers that existing products should be taken off the shelf to make room for a new one without any sales history is not easy. As retailers become more sophisticated, the task may become even more difficult.

Sales promotion, in the form of trade promotion, is a virtual necessity to obtain the necessary trade cooperation. The trade requires additional incentive to accept the risk to their profit that a new product poses. The requirements for trade promotion in the introduction of a new product add considerably to the cost of the new product introduction.

Getting Trial　Once the distribution is obtained, the manufacturer must get the consumer to try it. Several sales promotion methods can be used for the purpose, including both sampling and coupons. Providing free samples of the new product, or attractive price offers, can be very expensive. Not only is the manufacturer faced with substantial trade promotion expense, but also with substantial consumer promotion expense.

Encouraging Repeat Purchasing　Sales promotion can be quite effective in getting the initial consumer experience with the new product, but success is still not guaranteed. Most products, new or established, find themselves in an extremely competitive environment. Competitors continue with their promotional programs, and they likely have the advantage of more than one trial experience.

A new product must also be promoted to encourage repeat purchasing even after a trial has been obtained. Additional couponing and other promotional efforts must continue to be employed to encourage repeat purchasing. A new product introduction then requires trade promotion to obtain distribution, consumer promotion to obtain consumer product trial, and more trade and consumer promotion to encourage repeat product purchasing in the competitive environment where most products are found.

Case: Colas 1

Reviewing trade promotional activity on an event by event basis usually leads to the conclusion that more promotion generates more volume and consequently more revenue. As long as the promoted cases are sold at prices above the variable cost of production and distribution, they make a contribution to profit and overhead. In this case, the consequences of an increasing rate of promotion in a market will be examined.

Background　Cola sales in all major grocery outlets in a market were collected using supermarket scanners. Information about the type of trade promotion was collected to determine sales with in-store display only, feature ad only, and combination of feature ad with in-store display. Table 4-1 shows volume movements and prices under these various conditions for the dominant pack sizes of Coke and Pepsi. These pack sizes account for about 80 percent of cola sales in the city. Prices are given on a standard unit basis, and not on the actual shelf prices of the dominant package size. In Table 4-2, volumes have been normalized for differences in overall store sales that occur from cell to cell and week to week (volume per $1,000 All Commodity Volume).

Table 4-3 gives four-week moving averages for several key variables in the case. (Refer to the following case for the general background on the cola product category.)

Table 4-1
CITY SALES OF DOMINANT COLA PACKS BY WEEK
PRICE IS VOLUME WEIGHTED AVERAGE
SALES BY PROMOTIONAL TYPE
--BRAND=PEPSI------------------------------------

WEEK	TOTAL VOLUME	VOL W/NO PROMO	PRICE W/NO PROMO	VOL WITH DISPL ONLY	PRICE WITH DISPL ONLY	VOL WITH FEAT ONLY	PRICE WITH FEAT ONLY	VOL WITH FEAT & DISPL	PRICE WITH FEAT & DISPL
1	6915.3	3524.4	3.31	0.0	.	3390.9	2.90	0.0	.
2	7265.9	1039.9	4.11	0.0	.	6226.0	2.55	0.0	.
3	6843.5	2904.0	2.81	0.0	.	3939.5	2.58	0.0	.
4	9449.7	2136.9	2.40	0.0	.	7312.8	2.69	0.0	.
5	7541.6	1020.8	4.05	0.0	.	6520.8	2.70	0.0	.
6	8065.2	2619.5	2.83	0.0	.	5445.7	2.88	0.0	.
7	6651.3	3077.1	2.95	0.0	.	3574.3	2.57	0.0	.
8	9081.6	2090.0	2.63	0.0	.	6991.6	2.97	0.0	.
9	9882.4	3148.9	3.24	0.0	.	6733.5	2.10	0.0	.
10	10925.2	569.1	3.81	0.0	.	10356.1	2.82	0.0	.
11	6833.2	1402.1	4.58	0.0	.	5431.1	2.49	0.0	.
12	8577.1	946.0	5.20	0.0	.	7631.1	2.66	0.0	.
13	10416.3	3807.5	2.89	0.0	.	6608.8	3.02	0.0	.
14	12274.5	6938.8	2.42	0.0	.	5335.7	1.74	0.0	.
15	13597.5	3712.1	3.23	0.0	.	9885.3	3.13	0.0	.
16	14855.9	885.9	3.22	0.0	.	13970.0	1.87	0.0	.
17	13381.9	2273.3	2.79	0.0	.	11108.5	2.02	0.0	.
18	13688.4	2754.4	3.29	0.0	.	10934.0	1.89	0.0	.
19	12183.6	2233.7	3.30	0.0	.	9949.9	2.26	0.0	.
20	12207.1	4314.9	2.82	0.0	.	7892.1	2.57	0.0	.
21	13233.7	4952.9	2.51	0.0	.	8280.8	3.16	0.0	.
22	8800.0	4193.2	3.45	0.0	.	4606.8	3.31	0.0	.
23	10158.1	4760.8	2.75	0.0	.	5397.3	3.45	0.0	.
24	10059.9	5850.5	3.36	0.0	.	4209.3	3.18	0.0	.
25	9518.7	6655.7	3.45	0.0	.	2862.9	3.44	0.0	.
26	11959.2	4658.1	3.14	0.0	.	7301.1	2.94	0.0	.
27	12537.1	5472.1	2.93	0.0	.	7064.9	2.91	0.0	.
28	10564.4	7604.7	3.10	0.0	.	2959.7	2.89	0.0	.
29	9172.5	4489.5	3.44	0.0	.	2471.3	3.32	2211.7	3.30
30	10658.3	6990.1	3.05	0.0	.	3668.1	3.05	0.0	.
31	14442.3	2846.8	2.73	0.0	.	6129.2	2.94	5466.3	2.89
32	12295.1	12295.1	3.02	0.0	.	0.0	.	0.0	.
33	11095.3	7868.7	3.08	0.0	.	3226.7	2.89	0.0	.
34	12274.5	7588.5	2.86	0.0	.	4686.0	3.10	0.0	.
35	11652.7	7477.1	3.22	0.0	.	4175.6	3.20	0.0	.
36	10762.4	9911.7	2.99	0.0	.	850.7	2.80	0.0	.
37	10964.8	3682.8	3.03	0.0	.	5410.5	2.90	1871.5	3.03
38	9861.9	8798.5	3.04	0.0	.	1063.3	2.63	0.0	.

Table 4-1 (CONTINUED)

---BRAND=PEPSI--

WEEK	TOTAL VOLUME	VOL W/NO PROMO	PRICE W/NO PROMO	VOL WITH DISPL ONLY	PRICE WITH DISPL ONLY	VOL WITH FEAT ONLY	PRICE WITH FEAT ONLY	VOL WITH FEAT & DISPL	PRICE WITH FEAT & DISPL
39	12144.0	3597.7	3.03	0.0	.	4081.7	2.79	4464.5	2.94
40	11595.5	7343.6	3.09	0.0	.	2987.6	2.89	1264.2	2.57
41	11517.7	7617.9	3.10	0.0	.	2911.3	2.90	988.5	2.61
42	13466.9	3373.3	3.44	0.0	.	7846.7	2.41	2246.9	2.02
43	11552.9	4668.4	3.43	941.6	3.41	5942.9	2.92	0.0	.
44	12258.4	1481.3	3.44	0.0	.	7834.9	2.73	2942.1	2.94
45	10714.0	3767.9	3.42	0.0	.	5126.0	2.87	1820.1	2.60
46	10115.6	3069.7	3.44	1770.3	3.44	5275.6	2.87	0.0	.
47	10802.0	2015.2	3.44	0.0	.	6849.3	2.89	1937.5	3.02
48	11591.1	3473.1	3.43	1207.1	3.44	6910.9	2.40	0.0	.
49	11671.7	995.9	3.44	0.0	.	8120.9	2.76	2554.9	2.99
50	10928.1	1060.4	3.44	0.0	.	9099.2	2.81	768.5	3.41
51	11156.9	932.8	3.44	0.0	.	6336.0	2.69	3888.1	3.18
52	11929.9	3470.1	3.44	2722.1	2.57	5537.6	2.85	0.0	.
53	13640.0	1268.7	3.44	0.0	.	5632.0	2.56	6739.3	2.83
54	10568.8	2447.9	3.44	1063.3	3.44	4983.7	2.58	2073.9	2.78
55	11472.3	966.5	3.44	0.0	.	4864.9	2.86	5740.8	2.72
56	9710.8	3081.5	3.44	0.0	.	6629.3	2.69	0.0	.
57	12852.4	1355.2	3.44	0.0	.	6974.0	2.44	4523.2	3.06
58	11526.5	2509.5	3.44	0.0	.	6312.5	3.00	2704.5	2.62
59	10639.2	2412.7	3.44	0.0	.	3581.6	2.72	4644.9	2.94
60	8751.6	3411.5	3.44	0.0	.	4734.4	2.66	605.7	3.43
61	13698.7	1186.5	3.44	0.0	.	5884.3	2.59	6627.9	2.51
62	9034.7	3316.1	3.44	0.0	.	5718.5	2.73	0.0	.
63	14536.1	0.0	.	0.0	.	8502.3	2.42	6033.9	2.39
64	11036.7	2522.7	3.36	0.0	.	8514.0	2.59	0.0	.
65	10807.9	0.0	.	0.0	.	7092.8	2.61	3715.1	3.30
66	9432.1	101.2	3.44	649.7	3.43	6312.5	3.06	2368.7	2.60
67	11041.1	2368.7	3.44	0.0	.	5721.5	2.59	2950.9	2.86
68	12620.7	0.0	.	0.0	.	8094.5	2.98	4526.1	3.06
69	10199.2	3845.6	3.44	0.0	.	3720.9	3.10	2632.7	2.96
70	11376.9	3666.7	3.44	0.0	.	6984.3	2.72	726.0	3.43
71	10851.9	1239.3	3.65	0.0	.	8112.1	3.01	1500.4	3.61
72	10100.9	1793.7	4.19	0.0	.	7060.5	2.95	1246.7	3.43
73	11332.9	0.0	.	0.0	.	8496.4	2.99	2836.5	3.23
74	10447.1	1922.8	4.27	0.0	.	7537.2	2.94	987.1	3.22
75	9234.1	1013.5	4.33	909.3	4.33	7311.3	3.08	0.0	.
76	10246.1	0.0	.	2849.7	3.44	7396.4	3.00	0.0	.
77	8364.6	1843.6	4.33	0.0	.	3816.3	3.49	2704.5	3.27
78	10423.6	3634.4	4.31	673.2	4.06	3414.4	2.97	2701.6	2.95
79	9091.9	2882.0	4.31	563.2	4.29	3175.3	2.96	2471.3	2.92

Table 4-1 (CONTINUED)
CITY SALES OF DOMINANT COLA PACKS BY WEEK
PRICE IS VOLUME WEIGHTED AVERAGE
SALES BY PROMOTIONAL TYPE

--BRAND=COKE--

WEEK	TOTAL VOLUME	VOL W/NO PROMO	PRICE W/NO PROMO	VOL WITH DISPL ONLY	PRICE WITH DISPL ONLY	VOL WITH FEAT ONLY	PRICE WITH FEAT ONLY	VOL WITH FEAT & DISPL	PRICE WITH FEAT & DISPL
1	5183.2	0.0	.	0.0	.	5183.2	3.07	0.0	.
2	3433.5	627.7	4.09	0.0	.	2805.7	2.56	0.0	.
3	3899.9	1563.5	2.85	0.0	.	2336.4	2.49	0.0	.
4	3157.7	423.9	4.11	0.0	.	2733.9	2.48	0.0	.
5	6309.6	0.0	.	0.0	.	6309.6	2.87	0.0	.
6	2710.4	1686.7	3.02	0.0	.	1023.7	2.59	0.0	.
7	8150.3	0.0	.	0.0	.	8150.3	2.50	0.0	.
8	3302.9	1129.3	3.91	0.0	.	2173.6	2.62	0.0	.
9	6170.3	199.5	3.81	0.0	.	5970.8	2.97	0.0	.
10	2892.3	649.7	4.05	0.0	.	2242.5	2.64	0.0	.
11	7016.5	0.0	.	0.0	.	7016.5	2.85	0.0	.
12	4304.7	1276.0	3.91	0.0	.	3028.7	2.60	0.0	.
13	4265.1	1306.8	3.46	0.0	.	2958.3	2.77	0.0	.
14	5595.3	67.5	3.46	0.0	.	5527.9	2.16	0.0	.
15	5344.5	3405.6	3.38	0.0	.	1938.9	3.12	0.0	.
16	6900.7	706.9	3.43	0.0	.	6193.7	1.92	0.0	.
17	6028.0	689.3	3.18	0.0	.	5338.7	2.04	0.0	.
18	6051.5	566.1	3.45	0.0	.	5485.3	1.91	0.0	.
19	5252.1	674.7	3.45	0.0	.	4577.5	2.40	0.0	.
20	4338.4	1723.3	3.01	0.0	.	2615.1	2.32	0.0	.
21	6358.0	3134.3	2.56	0.0	.	3223.7	3.01	0.0	.
22	6668.9	1704.3	2.69	0.0	.	4964.7	3.43	0.0	.
23	3982.0	1837.7	3.45	0.0	.	2144.3	3.35	0.0	.
24	4696.3	3223.7	3.36	0.0	.	1472.5	3.09	0.0	.
25	4488.0	3147.5	3.45	156.9	3.523	1183.6	3.44	0.0	.
26	5470.7	2725.1	3.14	0.0	.	2745.6	2.89	0.0	.
27	4451.3	3143.1	3.36	0.0	.	1308.3	3.36	0.0	.
28	6283.2	985.6	2.57	206.8	3.436	5090.8	3.20	0.0	.
29	3936.5	2670.8	3.36	0.0	.	1039.9	3.35	225.9	3.44
30	6369.7	1218.8	2.68	0.0	.	4004.0	2.59	1146.9	2.88
31	4628.8	1488.7	3.01	479.6	3.43	2660.5	2.80	0.0	.
32	5654.0	792.0	2.75	0.0	.	2496.3	2.70	2365.7	2.95
33	4829.7	1604.5	3.26	0.0	.	3225.2	2.84	0.0	.
34	4744.7	2032.8	3.12	0.0	.	2711.9	2.90	0.0	.
35	5005.7	2068.0	3.14	0.0	.	2937.7	3.32	0.0	.
36	6369.7	2644.4	2.76	0.0	.	2556.4	2.87	1168.9	2.90
37	4134.5	2752.9	3.18	0.0	.	1381.6	2.86	0.0	.
38	5922.4	668.8	3.44	0.0	.	4228.4	2.83	1025.2	2.95

Table 4-1 (CONTINUED)

---BRAND=COKE--

WEEK	TOTAL VOLUME	VOL W/NO PROMO	PRICE W/NO PROMO	VOL WITH DISPL ONLY	PRICE WITH DISPL ONLY	VOL WITH FEAT ONLY	PRICE WITH FEAT ONLY	VOL WITH FEAT & DISPL	PRICE WITH FEAT & DISPL
39	4734.4	3213.5	3.15	0.0	.	1520.9	2.81	0.0	.
40	6113.1	224.4	2.84	897.6	3.44	3685.7	2.82	1305.3	2.91
41	4900.1	1660.3	3.31	511.9	3.44	2728.0	2.78	0.0	.
42	7466.8	711.3	3.44	0.0	.	4102.3	2.37	2653.2	2.56
43	5662.8	2862.9	3.50	0.0	.	2799.9	2.91	0.0	.
44	4919.2	1717.5	3.44	0.0	.	3201.7	2.92	0.0	.
45	6426.9	623.3	3.44	0.0	.	3097.6	2.81	2706.0	2.90
46	4787.2	2334.9	3.43	0.0	.	2452.3	2.87	0.0	.
47	4122.8	1893.5	3.44	0.0	.	2229.3	2.85	0.0	.
48	6010.4	610.1	3.44	0.0	.	5400.3	2.84	0.0	.
49	4892.8	1708.7	3.44	0.0	.	3184.1	2.79	0.0	.
50	5266.8	1669.1	3.44	0.0	.	3597.7	2.63	0.0	.
51	4794.5	1669.1	3.44	0.0	.	3125.5	2.78	0.0	.
52	6113.1	1010.5	3.44	0.0	.	4115.5	2.73	987.1	2.96
53	4894.3	2255.7	3.43	0.0	.	2638.5	2.67	0.0	.
54	5472.1	844.8	3.44	0.0	.	4627.3	2.83	0.0	.
55	5159.7	459.1	3.44	0.0	.	4571.6	2.75	129.1	3.44
56	8185.5	0.0	.	0.0	.	4807.7	2.88	3377.7	2.72
57	4941.2	884.4	3.44	0.0	.	4056.8	2.67	0.0	.
58	4608.3	1713.1	3.44	0.0	.	2895.2	2.66	0.0	.
59	5854.9	573.5	3.44	0.0	.	5145.1	2.73	136.4	3.44
60	4970.5	488.4	3.44	0.0	.	2070.9	2.66	2411.2	2.71
61	4505.6	1760.0	3.44	0.0	.	2745.6	2.64	0.0	.
62	6173.2	0.0	.	0.0	.	4030.4	3.01	2142.8	2.93
63	4357.5	0.0	.	0.0	.	4357.5	2.98	0.0	.
64	5915.1	451.7	3.10	0.0	.	4109.6	2.78	1353.7	2.68
65	4675.7	2029.9	3.44	0.0	.	2645.9	2.99	0.0	.
66	6542.8	0.0	.	0.0	.	5705.3	2.55	837.5	3.31
67	5953.2	0.0	.	0.0	.	3462.8	2.73	2490.4	2.98
68	5149.5	2197.1	3.41	0.0	.	2952.4	2.99	0.0	.
69	7004.8	577.9	3.44	0.0	.	6426.9	2.73	0.0	.
70	6831.7	709.9	3.44	0.0	.	2939.2	2.70	3182.7	2.96
71	5155.3	2103.2	3.42	0.0	.	3052.1	2.90	0.0	.
72	7362.7	714.3	3.44	0.0	.	2600.4	2.83	4048.0	3.12
73	4930.9	2186.8	3.42	0.0	.	2744.1	2.85	0.0	.
74	6976.9	671.7	3.60	0.0	.	2579.9	2.80	3725.3	2.60
75	4652.3	1806.9	4.01	0.0	.	2845.3	3.03	0.0	.
76	4499.7	1696.9	4.01	0.0	.	1441.7	3.23	1361.1	2.79
77	6120.4	429.7	4.29	0.0	.	1386.0	3.47	4304.7	2.94
78	5370.9	2563.7	3.73	0.0	.	2807.2	3.03	0.0	.
79	6710.0	123.2	5.20	533.9	3.97	1267.2	2.98	4785.7	3.00

Table 4-2
CITY SALES OF DOMINANT COLA PACKS BY WEEK
PRICE IS VOLUME WEIGHTED AVERAGE
NORMALIZED SALES BY PROMOTIONAL TYPE
0 = NO PROMO, D = DISPLAY ONLY, F = FEATURE ONLY, C = COMBINED

--BRAND=PEPSI--

WEEK	TOTAL VOLUME	VOL W/NO PROMO	PRICE W/NO PROMO	VOL WITH DISPL ONLY	PRICE WITH DISPL ONLY	VOL WITH FEAT ONLY	PRICE WITH FEAT ONLY	VOL WITH FEAT & DISPL	PRICE WITH FEAT & DISPL
1	9.7	7.7	3.31	0.0	.	13.0	2.90	0.0	.
2	10.0	4.1	4.11	0.0	.	13.3	2.55	0.0	.
3	10.6	9.1	2.81	0.0	.	12.0	2.58	0.0	.
4	14.6	18.4	2.40	0.0	.	13.8	2.69	0.0	.
5	9.7	3.3	4.05	0.0	.	13.9	2.70	0.0	.
6	12.3	10.6	2.83	0.0	.	13.2	2.88	0.0	.
7	9.5	7.5	2.95	0.0	.	12.1	2.57	0.0	.
8	13.0	17.8	2.63	0.0	.	12.1	2.97	0.0	.
9	12.0	6.7	3.24	0.0	.	18.9	2.10	0.0	.
10	15.0	4.8	3.81	0.0	.	17.0	2.82	0.0	.
11	10.0	3.5	4.58	0.0	.	18.9	2.49	0.0	.
12	14.3	4.4	5.20	0.0	.	19.9	2.66	0.0	.
13	13.0	14.2	2.89	0.0	.	12.4	3.02	0.0	.
14	15.7	11.7	2.42	0.0	.	28.3	1.74	0.0	.
15	16.6	7.5	3.23	0.0	.	30.8	3.13	0.0	.
16	18.9	8.2	3.22	0.0	.	20.6	1.87	0.0	.
17	15.8	10.6	2.79	0.0	.	17.6	2.02	0.0	.
18	14.8	10.0	3.29	0.0	.	16.9	1.89	0.0	.
19	15.1	9.3	3.30	0.0	.	17.5	2.26	0.0	.
20	16.1	10.9	2.82	0.0	.	21.9	2.57	0.0	.
21	16.0	12.5	2.51	0.0	.	19.3	3.16	0.0	.
22	9.4	6.7	3.45	0.0	.	14.8	3.31	0.0	.
23	14.1	13.0	2.75	0.0	.	15.2	3.45	0.0	.
24	13.0	10.8	3.36	0.0	.	18.0	3.18	0.0	.
25	11.9	10.6	3.45	0.0	.	16.5	3.44	0.0	.
26	12.8	9.0	3.14	0.0	.	17.5	2.94	0.0	.
27	16.1	15.2	2.93	0.0	.	16.8	2.91	0.0	.
28	14.5	12.7	3.10	0.0	.	22.7	2.89	0.0	.
29	12.6	9.3	3.44	0.0	.	19.1	3.32	19.2	3.30
30	13.9	12.5	3.05	0.0	.	17.8	3.05	0.0	.
31	17.1	11.7	2.73	0.0	.	19.4	2.94	19.0	2.89
32	16.5	16.5	3.02	0.0	.	0.0	.	0.0	.
33	14.8	12.7	3.08	0.0	.	24.7	2.89	0.0	.
34	16.1	18.2	2.86	0.0	.	13.6	3.10	0.0	.
35	13.1	11.6	3.22	0.0	.	17.0	3.29	0.0	.
36	14.4	14.7	2.99	0.0	.	11.4	2.80	0.0	.
37	14.9	13.3	3.03	0.0	.	17.0	2.90	13.2	3.03
38	12.6	12.5	3.04	0.0	.	13.2	2.63	0.0	.

Table 4-2 (CONTINUED)

---BRAND=PEPSI---

WEEK	TOTAL VOLUME	VOL W/NO PROMO	PRICE W/NO PROMO	VOL WITH DISPL ONLY	PRICE WITH DISPL ONLY	VOL WITH FEAT ONLY	PRICE WITH FEAT ONLY	VOL WITH FEAT & DISPL	PRICE WITH FEAT & DISPL
39	13.8	11.0	3.03	0.0	.	19.9	2.79	12.7	2.94
40	14.8	12.2	3.09	0.0	.	23.4	2.89	23.3	2.57
41	14.8	12.8	3.10	0.0	.	22.7	2.90	18.4	2.61
42	18.4	8.2	3.44	0.0	.	29.0	2.41	45.0	2.02
43	13.8	8.7	3.43	22.6	3.41	22.7	2.92	0.0	.
44	15.0	8.1	3.44	0.0	.	20.1	2.73	12.0	2.94
45	14.2	8.6	3.42	0.0	.	22.3	2.87	21.0	2.60
46	13.5	9.8	3.44	8.8	3.44	22.3	2.87	0.0	.
47	15.3	9.2	3.44	0.0	.	19.9	2.89	13.6	3.02
48	12.6	7.3	3.43	8.5	3.44	23.0	2.40	0.0	.
49	15.0	6.0	3.44	0.0	.	18.3	2.76	15.3	2.99
50	13.9	6.4	3.44	0.0	.	15.7	2.81	19.0	3.41
51	14.6	5.8	3.44	0.0	.	22.4	2.69	12.1	3.18
52	13.1	6.7	3.44	25.0	2.57	20.3	2.85	0.0	.
53	16.3	7.1	3.44	0.0	.	21.9	2.56	16.9	2.83
54	13.2	7.8	3.44	6.7	3.44	20.3	2.58	24.2	2.78
55	14.5	6.5	3.44	0.0	.	17.5	2.86	15.5	2.72
56	12.3	6.5	3.44	0.0	.	21.2	2.69	0.0	.
57	13.9	6.8	3.44	0.0	.	21.0	2.44	11.6	3.06
58	14.4	7.8	3.44	0.0	.	17.2	3.00	24.6	2.62
59	13.3	7.7	3.44	0.0	.	20.7	2.72	15.0	2.94
60	11.3	7.4	3.44	0.0	.	17.2	2.66	15.4	3.43
61	14.4	5.9	3.44	0.0	.	17.1	2.59	16.3	2.51
62	11.3	7.1	3.44	0.0	.	17.0	2.73	0.0	.
63	17.5	0.0	.	0.0	.	18.6	2.42	16.0	2.39
64	14.3	8.2	3.36	0.0	.	18.3	2.59	0.0	.
65	12.0	0.0	.	0.0	.	13.3	2.61	10.1	3.30
66	10.9	1.9	3.44	13.7	3.43	9.7	3.06	20.0	2.60
67	13.2	7.3	3.44	0.0	.	16.3	2.59	18.0	2.86
68	14.0	0.0	.	0.0	.	15.5	2.98	12.0	3.06
69	13.5	8.9	3.44	0.0	.	17.8	3.10	22.2	2.96
70	12.2	7.2	3.44	0.0	.	19.2	2.72	13.2	3.43
71	13.3	8.5	3.65	0.0	.	16.2	3.01	8.8	3.61
72	12.2	5.9	4.19	0.0	.	14.7	2.95	29.2	3.43
73	14.0	0.0	.	0.0	.	14.1	2.99	13.8	3.23
74	10.7	5.8	4.27	0.0	.	12.9	2.94	16.1	3.22
75	11.1	6.1	4.33	6.7	4.33	13.8	3.08	0.0	.
76	13.0	0.0	.	10.0	3.44	14.7	3.00	0.0	.
77	10.6	6.3	4.33	0.0	.	11.2	3.49	17.1	3.27
78	10.8	6.3	4.31	10.5	4.06	18.5	2.97	19.2	2.95
79	10.8	5.7	4.31	11.2	4.29	19.4	2.96	19.4	2.92

Table 4-2 (CONTINUED)
CITY SALES OF DOMINANT COLA PACKS BY WEEK
PRICE IS VOLUME WEIGHTED AVERAGE
NORMALIZED SALES BY PROMOTIONAL TYPE
0 = NO PROMO, D = DISPLAY ONLY, F = FEATURE ONLY, C = COMBINED

--BRAND=COKE--

WEEK	TOTAL VOLUME	VOL W/NO PROMO	PRICE W/NO PROMO	VOL WITH DISPL ONLY	PRICE WITH DISPL ONLY	VOL WITH FEAT ONLY	PRICE WITH FEAT ONLY	VOL WITH FEAT & DISPL	PRICE WITH FEAT & DISPL
1	7.2	0.0	.	0.0	.	7.2	3.07	0.0	.
2	4.8	2.4	4.09	0.0	.	6.0	2.56	0.0	.
3	6.0	4.9	2.85	0.0	.	7.1	2.49	0.0	.
4	4.9	1.8	4.11	0.0	.	6.6	2.48	0.0	.
5	8.1	0.0	.	0.0	.	8.1	2.87	0.0	.
6	4.1	3.5	3.02	0.0	.	5.9	2.59	0.0	.
7	11.6	0.0	.	0.0	.	11.6	2.50	0.0	.
8	4.7	2.7	3.91	0.0	.	7.8	2.62	0.0	.
9	7.5	1.4	3.81	0.0	.	8.7	2.97	0.0	.
10	4.0	2.0	4.05	0.0	.	5.5	2.64	0.0	.
11	10.2	0.0	.	0.0	.	10.2	2.85	0.0	.
12	7.2	3.9	3.91	0.0	.	11.2	2.60	0.0	.
13	5.3	3.0	3.46	0.0	.	8.0	2.77	0.0	.
14	7.2	1.0	3.46	0.0	.	7.8	2.16	0.0	.
15	6.5	5.3	3.38	0.0	.	11.4	3.12	0.0	.
16	8.8	3.5	3.43	0.0	.	10.6	1.92	0.0	.
17	7.1	3.2	3.18	0.0	.	8.4	2.04	0.0	.
18	6.6	2.1	3.45	0.0	.	8.5	1.91	0.0	.
19	6.5	2.8	3.45	0.0	.	8.1	2.40	0.0	.
20	5.7	3.5	3.01	0.0	.	10.0	2.32	0.0	.
21	7.7	7.2	2.56	0.0	.	8.3	3.01	0.0	.
22	7.1	4.9	2.69	0.0	.	8.5	3.43	0.0	.
23	5.5	3.8	3.45	0.0	.	9.2	3.35	0.0	.
24	6.1	5.2	3.36	0.0	.	9.5	3.09	0.0	.
25	5.6	5.3	3.45	4.7	3.52	6.8	3.44	0.0	.
26	5.9	4.3	3.14	0.0	.	8.9	2.89	0.0	.
27	5.7	5.5	3.36	0.0	.	6.3	3.36	0.0	.
28	8.6	5.0	2.57	5.1	3.44	10.4	3.20	0.0	.
29	5.4	5.1	3.36	0.0	.	6.4	3.35	5.8	3.44
30	8.3	4.6	2.68	0.0	.	10.3	2.59	10.0	2.88
31	5.5	3.8	3.01	3.3	3.43	8.7	2.80	0.0	.
32	7.6	4.3	2.75	0.0	.	9.2	2.70	8.1	2.95
33	6.5	3.7	3.26	0.0	.	10.1	2.84	0.0	.
34	6.2	4.4	3.12	0.0	.	8.9	2.90	0.0	.
35	5.6	4.0	3.14	0.0	.	8.0	3.32	0.0	.
36	8.5	9.5	2.76	0.0	.	7.8	2.87	8.4	2.90
37	5.6	5.1	3.18	0.0	.	7.0	2.86	0.0	.
38	7.5	3.6	3.44	0.0	.	9.0	2.83	7.9	2.95

Table 4-2 (CONTINUED)

---BRAND=COKE---

WEEK	TOTAL VOLUME	VOL W/NO PROMO	PRICE W/NO PROMO	VOL WITH DISPL ONLY	PRICE WITH DISPL ONLY	VOL WITH FEAT ONLY	PRICE WITH FEAT ONLY	VOL WITH FEAT & DISPL	PRICE WITH FEAT & DISPL
39	5.4	4.8	3.15	0.0	.	7.0	2.81	0.0	.
40	7.8	5.1	2.84	5.0	3.44	8.9	2.82	9.0	2.91
41	6.3	4.7	3.31	3.9	3.44	9.4	2.78	0.0	.
42	10.2	4.7	3.44	0.0	.	12.8	2.37	10.1	2.56
43	6.8	5.0	3.50	0.0	.	10.7	2.92	0.0	.
44	6.0	3.7	3.44	0.0	.	9.0	2.92	0.0	.
45	8.5	3.8	3.44	0.0	.	9.8	2.81	9.8	2.90
46	6.4	4.6	3.43	0.0	.	10.4	2.87	0.0	.
47	5.8	4.0	3.44	0.0	.	9.7	2.85	0.0	.
48	6.5	2.8	3.44	0.0	.	7.7	2.84	0.0	.
49	6.3	3.9	3.44	0.0	.	9.3	2.79	0.0	.
50	6.7	3.8	3.44	0.0	.	10.5	2.63	0.0	.
51	6.3	3.9	3.44	0.0	.	9.3	2.78	0.0	.
52	6.7	3.3	3.44	0.0	.	9.1	2.73	6.7	2.96
53	5.9	3.9	3.43	0.0	.	10.2	2.67	0.0	.
54	6.8	3.5	3.44	0.0	.	8.3	2.83	0.0	.
55	6.5	3.1	3.44	0.0	.	7.6	2.75	3.4	3.44
56	10.4	0.0	.	0.0	.	11.3	2.88	9.2	2.72
57	5.4	2.9	3.44	0.0	.	6.6	2.67	0.0	.
58	5.8	3.6	3.44	0.0	.	8.9	2.66	0.0	.
59	7.3	3.6	3.44	0.0	.	8.6	2.73	3.5	3.44
60	6.7	3.3	3.44	0.0	.	7.5	2.66	7.7	2.71
61	4.7	3.2	3.44	0.0	.	6.9	2.64	0.0	.
62	8.1	0.0	.	0.0	.	9.2	3.01	6.7	2.93
63	5.2	0.0	.	0.0	.	5.2	2.98	0.0	.
64	7.7	3.3	3.10	0.0	.	9.0	2.78	7.5	2.68
65	5.2	3.3	3.44	0.0	.	9.0	2.99	0.0	.
66	7.5	0.0	.	0.0	.	8.1	2.55	5.0	3.31
67	7.1	0.0	.	0.0	.	6.7	2.73	7.7	2.98
68	5.7	4.6	3.41	0.0	.	7.0	2.99	0.0	.
69	9.2	4.1	3.44	0.0	.	10.4	2.73	0.0	.
70	7.4	3.7	3.44	0.0	.	8.1	2.70	8.4	2.96
71	6.3	4.6	3.42	0.0	.	8.4	2.90	0.0	.
72	8.9	4.3	3.44	0.0	.	8.3	2.83	11.7	3.12
73	6.1	4.3	3.42	0.0	.	9.2	2.85	0.0	.
74	7.1	2.4	3.60	0.0	.	8.4	2.80	9.4	2.60
75	5.6	3.8	4.01	0.0	.	8.1	3.03	0.0	.
76	5.7	3.8	4.01	0.0	.	6.3	3.23	11.6	2.79
77	7.7	2.8	4.29	0.0	.	6.1	3.47	10.5	2.94
78	5.5	4.0	3.73	0.0	.	8.6	3.03	0.0	.
79	7.9	2.4	5.20	2.9	3.97	7.7	2.98	10.8	3.00

Table 4-3
4 WEEK MOVING AVERAGES
---BRAND=PEPSI---

WEEK	PROMO OPPORTUNITY	ADJUSTED $ SALES	TOTAL VOLUME	NO PROMO VOLUME	FEAT ONLY VOLUME
4	58.400	31.1429	11.2275	9.8317	13.0472
5	64.400	30.6410	11.2375	8.7275	13.2616
6	63.900	32.4501	11.7900	10.3670	13.2349
7	61.675	31.8542	11.5075	9.9657	13.2630
8	61.975	31.6329	11.1025	9.8102	12.8217
9	57.700	32.0231	11.6750	10.6648	14.0645
10	62.975	34.0419	12.3675	9.2075	15.0146
11	62.950	34.8155	12.4925	8.2020	16.7205
12	58.150	35.9431	12.8125	4.8472	18.6794
13	64.000	38.2245	13.0650	6.7182	17.0543
14	49.150	35.8030	13.2400	8.4529	19.8639
15	48.500	41.6718	14.9075	9.4415	22.8434
16	54.075	40.3610	16.0625	10.4071	23.0261
17	56.075	39.2033	16.7650	9.5007	24.3275
18	67.550	38.8935	16.5375	9.0660	21.4753
19	75.300	35.0091	16.1500	9.5219	18.1455
20	65.625	36.5108	15.4500	10.1773	18.4667
21	60.000	39.7043	15.5075	10.6632	18.8859
22	50.775	39.5840	14.1550	9.8441	18.3752
23	45.525	41.3167	13.9050	10.7701	17.7933
24	41.150	41.2378	13.1150	10.7488	16.8250
25	33.550	39.7812	12.0800	10.2721	16.1329
26	36.375	41.4980	12.9250	10.8403	16.8077
27	37.525	42.2470	13.4250	11.3881	17.2159
28	34.475	42.6562	13.8150	11.8773	18.3818
29	37.500	43.0807	14.0025	11.5884	19.0279
30	33.100	44.0414	14.2850	12.4353	19.0943
31	37.475	44.5975	14.5325	11.5726	19.7281
32	33.000	45.9856	15.0225	12.5073	14.0546
33	28.925	46.5463	15.5700	13.3573	15.4595
34	33.525	47.8144	16.1150	14.7835	14.4021
35	22.625	46.1586	15.1250	14.7574	13.8042
36	25.125	44.4454	14.6075	14.3243	16.6567
37	36.400	44.2452	14.6175	14.4738	14.7217
38	27.650	41.7802	13.7325	13.0471	14.6247
39	36.450	41.1731	13.8950	12.8860	15.3455
40	39.750	41.4743	13.9900	12.2503	18.3413
41	29.975	41.6153	13.9825	12.1220	19.7789

Table 4-3 (CONTINUED)

---BRAND=PEPSI---

WEEK	PROMO OPPORTUNITY	ADJUSTED $ SALES	TOTAL VOLUME	NO PROMO VOLUME	FEAT ONLY VOLUME
42	38.325	44.1621	15.4400	11.0471	23.7395
43	31.675	45.0645	15.4525	10.4896	24.4489
44	45.300	44.7860	15.5050	9.4746	23.6152
45	49.875	44.3068	15.3375	8.4096	23.5163
46	53.525	42.9560	14.1200	8.8237	21.8464
47	61.700	43.5732	14.4975	8.9371	21.1540
48	54.275	41.7076	13.9025	8.7215	21.8995
49	63.525	41.8037	14.1175	8.0900	20.8913
50	68.700	41.3106	14.2150	7.2348	19.2268
51	71.225	40.4287	14.0325	6.3957	19.8368
52	69.975	41.2396	14.1575	6.2511	19.1571
53	69.900	41.7826	14.4775	6.5057	20.0521
54	65.400	41.2383	14.2950	6.8594	21.2059
55	65.925	40.8930	14.2825	7.0274	19.9998
56	65.075	40.1867	14.0725	6.9659	20.2128
57	65.000	38.4891	13.4800	6.8888	19.9968
58	64.675	39.7208	13.7850	6.8721	19.2171
59	59.550	39.3223	13.4850	7.1638	19.9974
60	59.750	38.8163	13.2275	7.3894	19.0035
61	59.925	38.6336	13.3425	7.1766	18.0324
62	55.500	36.2713	12.5650	7.0197	17.9927
63	65.325	36.8533	13.5950	5.0987	17.4793
64	70.300	38.2577	14.3575	5.3166	17.7539
65	75.575	37.3327	13.7525	3.8416	16.7933
66	88.575	36.9853	13.6500	2.5414	14.9689
67	78.925	35.8568	12.5825	4.3748	14.3903
68	88.850	36.5075	12.5100	2.3178	13.6855
69	74.650	38.7093	12.8775	4.5495	14.8254
70	62.400	39.7902	13.2200	5.8572	17.2067
71	67.575	40.9402	13.2450	6.1370	17.1805
72	58.400	40.2981	12.8025	7.6198	16.9894
73	72.600	40.2729	12.9475	5.3880	16.0623
74	77.850	39.6621	12.5550	5.0392	14.4752
75	77.325	38.4183	12.0100	4.4481	13.8836
76	86.500	38.6639	12.1975	2.9652	13.8822
77	77.275	37.4788	11.3300	4.5429	13.1446
78	70.825	38.3358	11.3500	4.6662	14.5480
79	60.925	38.3718	11.2650	4.5756	15.9461

Table 4-3 (CONTINUED)
4 WEEK MOVING AVERAGES

---BRAND=COKE---

WEEK	PROMO OPPORTUNITY	ADJUSTED $ SALES	TOTAL VOLUME	NO PROMO VOLUME	FEAT ONLY VOLUME
4	69.950	16.1904	5.7250	2.30255	6.7323
5	69.950	16.4564	5.9450	2.30255	6.9511
6	60.425	16.0332	5.7875	2.56156	6.9188
7	72.725	19.2837	7.1725	1.33252	8.0345
8	66.550	19.5978	7.1325	1.54251	8.3496
9	62.350	19.3928	6.9750	1.90187	8.4967
10	69.800	19.3891	6.9400	1.54120	8.3990
11	69.800	19.4393	6.6000	1.54120	8.0583
12	71.175	21.1837	7.2125	1.84157	8.8881
13	61.875	19.5326	6.6725	2.23708	8.7159
14	70.625	20.4827	7.4700	1.97222	9.2844
15	50.825	18.5768	6.5500	3.28657	9.5761
16	58.075	17.7662	6.9525	3.19120	9.4417
17	65.225	17.6681	7.4025	3.23843	9.5513
18	59.950	17.1382	7.2475	3.50639	9.7249
19	72.300	15.8948	7.2400	2.89293	8.8958
20	62.400	15.0582	6.4750	2.88649	8.7318
21	55.525	16.5568	6.6200	3.87852	8.6928
22	53.650	18.9588	6.7625	4.58116	8.6967
23	44.200	19.5303	6.5175	4.82194	8.9734
24	40.500	20.7722	6.5975	5.24834	8.8620
25	35.200	20.2497	6.0750	4.78061	8.4930
26	27.800	18.8982	5.7575	4.65235	8.5950
27	26.375	18.9912	5.8025	5.08372	7.8749
28	39.500	20.7523	6.4500	5.03033	8.1002
29	40.050	20.4763	6.4050	4.97704	8.0014
30	48.200	21.5907	7.0200	5.04606	8.3642
31	54.825	20.8220	6.9625	4.61187	8.9580
32	55.500	19.4331	6.6975	4.45162	8.6431
33	59.200	19.6742	6.9525	4.11095	9.5733
34	52.750	18.8001	6.4300	4.06103	9.2229
35	49.750	19.3552	6.4700	4.11045	9.0625
36	46.575	20.0572	6.7075	5.40365	8.7124
37	42.625	19.5606	6.4975	5.74387	7.9332
38	51.825	20.4032	6.8275	5.54796	7.9409
39	47.650	19.9094	6.7600	5.76447	7.6904
40	55.550	19.5883	6.5775	4.66119	7.9777
41	62.425	20.0594	6.7525	4.55582	8.5668

Table 4-3 (CONTINUED)
--BRAND=COKE--

WEEK	PROMO OPPORTUNITY	ADJUSTED $ SALES	TOTAL VOLUME	NO PROMO VOLUME	FEAT ONLY VOLUME
42	63.150	21.0258	7.4150	4.82998	9.5264
43	64.850	22.3889	7.7675	4.86949	10.4444
44	52.175	21.3417	7.3225	4.52866	10.4623
45	58.200	22.7409	7.8700	4.31005	10.5653
46	46.200	21.2972	6.9200	4.26404	9.9594
47	46.500	20.4173	6.6875	4.01374	9.7187
48	54.625	20.4914	6.8175	3.78034	9.4028
49	46.025	19.0611	6.2675	3.81201	9.2903
50	49.000	18.8758	6.3450	3.61159	9.3282
51	51.850	19.0280	6.4525	3.58933	9.2226
52	49.325	19.1349	6.4975	3.71038	9.5627
53	46.050	18.8090	6.3850	3.70444	9.7865
54	52.600	18.9586	6.4150	3.63176	9.2265
55	61.925	18.8655	6.4825	3.43391	8.7964
56	70.400	21.3085	7.3900	2.61374	9.3614
57	79.450	20.6528	7.2675	2.36675	8.4426
58	72.200	19.9039	7.0000	2.40145	8.5962
59	71.900	20.4467	7.2000	2.52569	8.8435
60	66.850	17.8006	6.2950	3.34292	7.8913
61	60.575	17.5345	6.1400	3.41071	7.9742
62	75.425	19.3599	6.7375	2.51058	8.0433
63	80.425	18.0949	6.2100	1.61246	7.2070
64	81.075	18.7764	6.4425	1.62841	7.5837
65	78.750	19.4029	6.5525	166804	8.1087
66	78.750	18.3342	6.4025	1.66804	7.8473
67	78.750	19.4730	6.8725	1.66804	8.2211
68	69.875	18.6800	6.3875	1.98205	7.7118
69	82.125	21.0037	7.4025	2.18183	8.0603
70	77.025	21.3299	7.3550	3.11807	8.0502
71	63.125	21.2068	7.1550	4.27564	8.4700
72	71.375	23.4750	7.9550	4.20312	8.7940
73	60.225	21.7606	7.1700	4.24166	8.4944
74	58.200	21.3682	7.1125	3.90730	8.5790
75	57.700	21.2187	6.9325	3.69229	8.4955
76	48.700	19.2538	6.1275	3.57619	7.9974
77	59.525	20.6119	6.5350	3.19170	7.2361
78	50.050	20.3444	6.1400	3.58466	7.2843
79	62.950	21.7644	6.7275	3.25330	7.2036

Table 4-1 gives city volume by promotion type. This table indicates the contribution of promotional activity to city sales, but since it is not adjusted for the size of the stores promoting in any given week, it provides little insight into the impact of promotional activity compared to base sales.

Table 4-2 is a normalization of Table 4-1 obtained by dividing the volume numbers in each column by a measure of the total store activity (shopper counts or total store sales) for stores running each promotional type. Tables of this type are useful for comparing the relative impact of any promotion type versus base sales, but do not indicate the overall importance of promotion to total brand sales.

Table 4-3 provides some four-week moving averages of key variables. The column headed "Promo Opportunity" is an indication of the degree of market coverage by promotion. For example, Pepsi shows a 58.4 in Week 4 "Promo Opportunity." This means that in the first four weeks, 58.4 percent of all grocery store dollar spending (all commodities) was spent in stores where there was an advertising feature, in-store display, or both on the Pepsi brand.

The adjusted dollar sales column gives an indication of the total retail sales revenue generated on the brand across all stores in the market. The three volume columns are adjusted for store sizes, and can be considered as proportional to brand volume sales per $1,000 total spent in the market in stores with the promotional conditions indicated.

Question 1   Without the aid of any computer statistical analysis techniques, trends and changes in these trends may be difficult to determine in the highly variable week-to-week scanner data. Two methods used to overcome this are moving averages and summarization over longer time periods.
a. Plot the percent of market covered by promotion for Coke from the four-week moving averages (Table 3)
b. Plot the percent of market covered by promotion for Coke from the four-week moving averages, but use only those weeks that are evenly divisible by 4
Contrast the results from these two plots in their ability to illustrate the degree of change over time in the data, and in their ease of interpretation.

Question 2   Both Coke and Pepsi exhibit significant variation in the percent of market covered by promotion across the time period considered. Plot from Table 4-3 the normalized volume on feature-only events versus percent coverage of market by promotion for the brand (promo opportunity). How does increasing the promotion frequency and coverage in this market affect the average sales on feature-only events?

Question 3   Plot for both Coke and Pepsi from Table 4-3 the normalized volume from non-promoting stores versus the percent promotion coverage of the market by the brand. How does increasing the promotion frequency in this market affect the average sales in non-promoting stores?

Question 4   For Coke from Table 4-2, plot normalized non-promoted volume versus the non-promoted price. Plot the feature-only volume versus the feature-only price. Discuss the relationship between price and volume shown in these plots.

Question 5   Plot from Table 4-3 the total normalized volume and total sales revenue for Coke versus the percent promotion coverage of the market. Repeat the plot for Pepsi. What do these graphs suggest about the relation between promotion coverage and total sales volume, and total retailer revenue from the brands?

Question 6 (Optional)   For students who have access to computerized regression analysis. Consider Coke from Tables 4-2 and 4-3, and use regression techniques to:
a. Relate non-promotion sales to non-promotion price
b. Relate non-promotion sales to promotion coverage
c. Relate non-promotion sales to both non-promotion price and promotion coverage
d. Relate feature-only sales to feature-only price
e. Relate feature-only sales to promotion coverage
f. Relate feature-only sales to both feature-only price and promotion coverage

Question 7 (Optional)   From the results in Question 6, compare Coke sales from Table 4-2 for the display-only events and the combination feature and display events to your best estimates of feature-only volume and non-promoted volume under similar conditions of pricing and promotion coverage. Discuss the results.

Case: Colas 2

Colas are sold through a variety of retail outlets, but this case considers only sales through grocery outlets. Around 90 percent of all households purchase a carbonated cola beverage at least once per year. This is based upon a sample of 10,000 households. The average time between purchases is about 37 days.

Background   The cola segment of carbonated beverages sold through grocery outlets is dominated by the Coca-Cola Company and by Pepsico, Inc. On an overall basis, including all diet and related products, each company holds about a 45 percent market share of total grocery sales. The business, however, is conducted through the operations of individual bottlers, both corporately operated and franchised. Market shares, prices, dominant package sizes, and levels of promotional activity vary widely from market to market.

Cola sales through grocery stores are one of the heaviest areas of trade promotion activity. About 67 percent of all cola sales are made with some form of trade promotion. About 40 percent of all cola sales are made with a feature price in an advertisement, 40 percent with an in-store display, and 40 percent with a shelf price reduction.

This case is based on cola sales, particularly Coke and Pepsi. In a chain of grocery outlets in a single market, sales data are collected by scanners. Nearly 80 percent of total cola sales are concentrated in a single dominant package size. This chain uses only two types of promotional support for Coke and Pepsi dominant packages, price reduction only and price reduction in conjunction with one additional element of trade support. Table 4-4 provides the data for this case. In addition to actual volume, an adjusted volume is given that removes fluctuations due to week-to-week variations in total store sales (volume per $1,000 All Commodity Volume normalization).

Table 4-4
CHAIN SALES OF DOMINANT COLA PACKS BY WEEK
SHARE IS VS DOMINANT COKE & PEPSI PACKS ONLY

	---COKE SALES---					
WEEK	**COKE ACTUAL VOLUME**	**COKE ADJUSTED VOLUME**	**COKE PRICE**	**COKE PROMO**	**COKE SHARE**	**LOG OF COKE VOL**
1	177.5	1.147	4.328		52	0.13715
2	142.3	0.908	4.328		43	−0.09651
3	127.6	0.855	4.328		43	−0.15665
4	360.8	2.299	3.241	YES	77	0.83247
5	379.9	2.378	3.241	YES	72	0.86626
6	102.7	0.680	4.328		20	−0.38566
7	124.7	0.824	4.328		21	−0.19358
8	409.2	2.717	3.241	YES	77	0.99953
9	404.8	2.302	3.241	YES	73	0.83378
10	547.1	3.481	3.241	YES	79	1.24732
11	99.7	0.653	4.328		13	−0.42618
12	98.3	0.689	4.328		15	−0.37251
13	536.8	3.098	3.241	YES	73	1.13076
14	117.3	0.707	4.328		17	−0.34672
15	114.4	0.703	4.328		15	−0.35240
16	404.8	2.874	3.241	YES	68	1.05570
17	529.5	3.506	3.241	YES	72	1.25448
18	142.3	0.844	4.328		17	−0.16960
19	780.3	4.708	3.154	YES	80	1.54926
20	174.5	1.097	4.328		21	0.09258
21	184.8	1.172	3.241		25	0.15871
22	838.9	4.484	3.001	YES	76	1.50052
23	715.7	4.343	3.241	YES	74	1.46857
24	243.5	1.591	4.328		50	0.46436
25	215.6	1.482	4.328		27	0.39339
26	862.4	4.918	2.980	YES	75	1.59290
27	225.9	1.416	4.459		47	0.34784
28	140.8	0.891	4.459		17	−0.11541
29	155.5	1.084	4.459		18	0.08066
30	705.5	4.159	3.241	YES	77	1.42527
31	736.3	4.250	3.345	YES	77	1.44692
32	189.2	1.200	4.459		26	0.18232
33	140.8	0.905	4.459		15	−0.09982
34	558.8	3.386	3.407	YES	72	1.21965
35	626.3	3.547	3.552	YES	77	1.26610
36	129.1	0.816	4.459		14	−0.20334
37	149.6	0.948	4.459		16	−0.05340
38	148.1	0.984	4.459		45	−0.01613
39	140.8	0.826	4.459		30	−0.19116

Table 4-4 (CONTINUED)

---COKE SALES---

WEEK	COKE ACTUAL VOLUME	COKE ADJUSTED VOLUME	COKE PRICE	COKE PROMO	COKE SHARE	LOG OF COKE VOL
40	129.1	0.822	4.459		18	−0.19601
41	132.0	0.888	4.459		19	−0.11878
42	140.8	0.957	4.459		39	−0.04395
43	137.9	0.867	4.459		38	−0.14272
44	105.6	0.659	4.459		17	−0.41703
45	586.7	4.132	3.219	YES	78	1.41876
46	186.3	1.243	4.459		22	0.21753
47	126.1	0.898	4.459		29	−0.10759
48	611.6	3.631	3.241	YES	79	1.28951
49	154.0	1.003	4.445		25	0.00300
50	123.2	0.779	4.459		16	−0.24974
51	635.1	4.018	3.241	YES	79	1.39078
52	181.9	1.127	4.459		45	0.11956
53	139.3	0.810	4.459		19	−0.21072
54	115.9	0.713	4.459		17	−0.33827
55	545.6	3.479	3.241	YES	71	1.24674
56	164.3	1.055	4.459		21	0.05354
57	158.4	0.903	4.763		19	−0.10203
58	462.0	2.854	3.821	YES	65	1.04872
59	646.8	4.206	3.299	YES	77	1.43651
60	171.6	1.095	4.490		20	0.09075
61	178.9	1.005	4.476		19	0.00499
62	594.0	3.755	3.297	YES	72	1.32309
62	176.0	1.119	4.763		20	0.11244
64	500.1	3.168	3.428	YES	62	1.15310
65	426.8	2.464	3.324	YES	51	0.90179
66	442.9	2.620	3.326	YES	51	0.96317
67	338.8	1.904	3.577	YES	33	0.64396
68	262.5	1.748	3.589	YES	39	0.55847
69	376.9	2.695	3.407		59	0.99140
70	435.6	2.518	3.528		57	0.92346
71	384.3	2.125	3.347	YES	46	0.75377
72	152.5	0.981	4.763		22	−0.01918
73	121.7	0.896	4.763		21	−0.10981
74	466.4	3.109	3.456	YES	72	1.13430
75	410.7	2.809	3.404	YES	68	1.03283
76	145.2	1.001	4.763		23	0.00100
77	136.4	1.001	4.763		23	0.00100
78	156.9	1.079	4.763		31	0.07603
79	375.5	2.593	3.479	YES	64	0.95282

Table 4-4 (CONTINUED)

---PEPSI SALES--

WEEK	PEPSI ACTUAL VOLUME	PEPSI ADJUSTED VOLUME	PEPSI PRICE	PEPSI PROMO	PEPSI SHARE	LOG OF PEPSI VOL	COKE MINUS PEPSI PRICE
1	161.3	1.04	4.328		48	0.04210	0.000
2	192.1	1.23	4.328		57	0.20376	0.000
3	167.2	1.12	4.328		57	0.11333	0.000
4	105.6	0.67	4.328		23	−0.39601	−1.087
5	151.1	0.95	4.328		28	−0.05551	−1.087
6	400.4	2.65	3.241	YES	80	0.97456	1.087
7	460.5	3.05	3.241	YES	79	1.11350	1.087
8	120.3	0.80	4.328		23	−0.22439	−1.087
9	151.1	0.86	4.328		27	−0.15199	−1.087
10	148.1	0.94	4.328		21	−0.05869	−1.087
11	658.5	4.31	3.263	YES	87	1.46140	1.065
12	561.7	3.94	3.255	YES	85	1.37118	1.073
13	202.4	1.17	4.328		27	0.15529	−1.087
14	592.5	3.57	3.241	YES	83	1.27257	1.087
15	639.5	3.93	3.241	YES	85	1.36915	1.087
16	187.7	1.33	4.328		32	0.28743	−1.087
17	209.7	1.39	4.328		28	0.32858	−1.087
18	704.0	4.18	3.254	YES	83	1.42983	1.074
19	198.0	1.20	4.328		20	0.17815	−1.174
20	664.4	4.18	3.342	YES	79	1.42959	0.986
21	550.0	3.49	3.434	YES	75	1.24904	−0.193
22	265.5	1.42	4.328		24	0.34995	−1.327
23	252.3	1.53	4.328		26	0.42592	−1.087
24	242.0	1.58	4.459		50	0.45806	−0.131
25	574.9	3.95	3.570	YES	73	1.37397	0.758
26	286.0	1.63	3.828		25	0.48919	−0.848
27	250.8	1.57	4.067		53	0.45298	0.392
28	695.2	4.40	3.356	YES	83	1.48183	1.103
29	695.2	4.85	3.380	YES	82	1.57877	1.079
30	214.1	1.26	4.459		23	0.23270	−1.218
31	224.4	1.30	4.459		23	025851	−1.114
32	529.5	3.36	3.592	YES	74	1.21105	0.867
33	783.2	5.04	3.343	YES	85	1.61661	1.116
34	215.6	1.31	4.459		28	0.26773	−1.052
35	186.3	1.06	4.459		23	0.05354	−0.907
36	767.1	4.85	3.114	YES	86	1.57836	1.345
37	774.4	4.91	3.108	YES	84	1.59026	1.351
38	177.5	1.18	4.399		55	0.16382	0.060
39	322.7	1.89	4.420		70	0.63816	0.039

Table 4-4 (CONTINUED)

------PEPSI SALES------

WEEK	PEPSI ACTUAL VOLUME	PEPSI ADJUSTED VOLUME	PEPSI PRICE	PEPSI PROMO	PEPSI SHARE	LOG OF PEPSI VOL	COKE MINUS PEPSI PRICE
40	599.9	3.82	3.091	YES	82	1.34025	1.368
41	577.9	3.89	3.142	YES	81	1.35789	1.317
42	220.0	1.50	4.459		61	0.40279	0.000
43	221.5	1.39	4.459		62	0.33146	0.000
44	513.3	3.20	3.150	YES	83	1.16409	1.309
45	170.1	1.20	4.459		22	0.18065	−1.240
46	649.7	4.34	3.301	YES	78	1.46672	1.158
47	312.4	2.22	3.612	YES	71	0.79931	0.847
48	164.3	0.98	4.404		21	−0.02532	−1.163
49	463.5	3.02	3.326	YES	75	1.10459	1.119
50	658.5	4.16	3.306	YES	84	1.42600	1.153
51	167.2	1.06	4.459		21	0.05638	−1.218
52	224.4	1.39	4.459		55	0.33002	0.000
53	586.7	3.41	3.338	YES	81	1.22730	1.121
54	547.1	3.37	3.316	YES	83	1.21432	1.143
55	220.0	1.40	4.459		29	0.33861	−1.218
56	623.3	4.00	3.642	YES	79	1.38704	0.817
57	689.3	3.93	3.351	YES	81	1.36838	1.412
58	243.5	1.50	4.690		35	0.40813	−0.869
59	196.5	1.28	4.684		23	0.24530	−1.385
60	695.2	4.44	3.337	YES	80	1.48975	1.153
61	752.4	4.23	3.315	YES	81	1.44126	1.161
62	234.7	1.48	4.763		28	0.39407	−1.466
63	708.4	4.51	3.064	YES	80	1.50519	1.699
64	305.1	1.93	3.609		38	0.65907	−0.181
65	413.6	2.39	3.574	YES	49	0.87046	−0.250
66	422.4	2.50	3.617	YES	49	0.91549	−0.291
67	683.5	3.84	2.904		67	1.34599	0.673
68	416.5	2.77	2.875		61	1.01993	0.714
69	266.9	1.91	3.645		41	0.64658	−0.238
70	331.5	1.92	3.672		43	0.65024	−0.144
71	442.9	2.45	3.575		54	0.89568	−0.228
72	529.5	3.41	3.318	YES	78	1.22524	1.445
73	469.3	3.46	3.319	YES	79	1.23982	1.444
74	178.9	1.19	4.763		28	0.17647	−1.307
75	193.6	1.32	4.763		32	0.28066	−1.359
76	495.7	3.42	3.308	YES	77	1.22935	1.455
77	460.5	3.38	3.313	YES	77	1.21758	1.450
78	353.5	2.43	4.056	YES	69	0.88830	0.707
79	208.3	1.44	4.763		36	0.36325	−1.284

The promotion column in Table 4-4 indicates if additional support was given beyond price reduction alone. Prices are given for a standardized unit and, while proportional to shelf prices per package, they are not the actual prices to which shoppers were exposed.

Question 1   Plot the Coke share by week. Use different symbols to indicate the following conditions:
a. No additional promotion support on either Coke or Pepsi
b. Support on Coke; no support on Pepsi
c. No support on Coke; support on Pepsi
d. Support on Coke, and support on Pepsi
What conclusions does this plot suggest about the relation of trade support to share of weekly sales?

Question 2   Plot Coke adjusted volume by week, again using four symbols to differentiate among the promotional support possibilities. What conclusions does this plot suggest about the relation of trade support to volume sales?

Question 3   Plot the total of Coke and Pepsi adjusted volumes by week, again using four symbols to differentiate among the promotional support possibilities. What conclusions does this plot suggest about the relation of trade support to total store movement?

Question 4   Weeks 36 through 44 were all non-promoted periods for Coke, but there were some Pepsi promotions. Make separate bar charts of the adjusted volume for Coke and Pepsi during these weeks. Indicate which weeks were Pepsi promotions. What do these charts indicate in terms of the sources of volume, of Pepsi promotion volume, and of the direct impact of Pepsi promotions on Coke sales?

Question 5   Plot Coke adjusted volume versus its price difference to Pepsi. What conclusions would you draw from this chart about the importance to Coke sales of price differentials to Pepsi?

Question 6   Plot Coke adjusted volume versus Coke price. Calculate the average adjusted volume for Coke at each different level of observed Coke price. Plot these averages. What conclusions would you draw from these charts about the importance to Coke sales of Coke's absolute price?

Question 7   Plot Coke share versus its price difference to Pepsi. What conclusions would you draw from this chart about the impact of price differentials to Pepsi on Coke's share?

Question 8   Plot Coke share versus Coke price. Comparing this chart to the chart from Question 7, which relation is strongest?

Question 9   Discuss the importance of price reductions and additional promotional activity to Coke's annual volume and share in this chain.

Case: Disposable Diapers

Disposable diapers are sold in drug stores, grocery stores, and mass merchandise outlets. The analysis conducted in this case is based on grocery stores only.

Background Trade promotion activity is fairly low, with about 15 percent of annual volume moved with trade deal activity. The average price reduction on trade deal is in the range of 5 percent to 10 percent. Manufacturer coupon activity is fairly

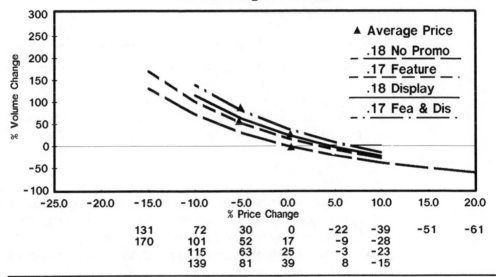

Figure 4-1
HUGGIES MEDIUM
PRICE/PROMOTION RESPONSE MODEL
The Marketing Fact Book™

	-25.0	-20.0	-15.0	-10.0	-5.0	0.0	5.0	10.0	15.0	20.0
			131	72	30	0	-22	-39	-51	-61
			170	101	52	17	-9	-28		
				115	63	25	-3	-23		
				139	81	39	8	-15		

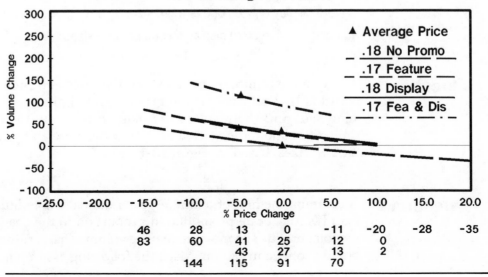

Figure 4-2
HUGGIES TODDLERS
PRICE/PROMOTION RESPONSE MODEL
The Marketing Fact Book™

	-25.0	-20.0	-15.0	-10.0	-5.0	0.0	5.0	10.0	15.0	20.0
			46	28	13	0	-11	-20	-28	-35
			83	60	41	25	12	0		
					43	27	13	2		
				144	115	91	70			

Table 4-5
DISPOSABLE DIAPERS BRAND SHARES

BRAND	CATEGORY SHARE	AVG. PROMO. PRICE PER UNIT
Pampers Mediums	17.5 %	15¢
Pampers Toddlers	13.0	19¢
Pampers Newborns	7.2	---
TOTAL PAMPERS	37.7 %	
Luvs Mediums	9.9	18¢
Luvs Toddlers	5.8	27¢
Luvs Newborns	2.4	---
TOTAL LUVS	18.1 %	
Huggies Mediums	14.1	18¢
Huggies Toddlers	9.1	26¢
Huggies Newborns	2.6	---
TOTAL HUGGIES	25.8 %	

high, with about 20 percent of volume sold associated with manufacturer coupon redemption. Table 4-5 shows category shares and average non-promoted prices for the major branded competitors.

An analysis was conducted to determine the response to pricing and retail promotion activity for the two major sizes of Huggies. Figure 4-1 and Figure 4-2 summarize the results of this analysis. Table 4-5 shows Huggies market share position. The size of the child determines the size of the disposable diaper required, so promotions do not cause any significant cross-size cannibalization. Promotions do not stimulate an appreciable increase in the product usage rate, so the primary sources of sales increases on promotion are from brand switchers, and from stockpiling purchase from brand-loyal users. The probability of finding any Huggies size on promotion in a grocery store is:

Promotion Condition	Percent of Weeks Occurring
No feature of display on any size (may have reduced shelf price or regular shelf price)	88.5
Ad feature only on one or more sizes	7.1
In-store display only on one or more sizes	3.4
Ad feature and in-store display on one or more sizes	1.0

Question 1   A common assumption in analyzing the price and promotion response for a brand is that all sizes of the brand react similarly. The dominant size is analyzed, and the results are assumed to apply to all sizes. Discuss the similarities and differences that exist in the price and promotion responses of the two sizes, based on Figures 4-1 and 4-2.

Question 2   A common method of allocating promotional expenditures among sizes of a brand is to allocate promotion in proportion to the share that the size has of the total brand. The measure may be volume share, revenue share, or share of brand profit contribution. Make the following assumptions:

a. The average retail mark-up is 25 percent of manufacturer list.
b. All incremental sales are the result of consumer sales shifted from competitive brands.
c. All promotion activity is in mediums and toddlers.
d. Forty percent of all Huggies promotional allowance offers to retailers result in shelf price reduction only, with complete retailer pass-through of the promotional allowance. The remaining 60 percent of Huggies promotional allowance offers result in retailer performance of feature only, display only, or both feature and displays.
e. The manufacturer of Huggies has the following promotional program: Once every two months, the retailer is allowed to purchase at 1-cent per diaper discount an amount of Huggies equal to three weeks sales of medium Huggies during periods with no ad feature or in-store display. Once every three months, the retailer is allowed to purchase at 1-cent per diaper discount an amount of Huggies toddlers equal to three weeks sales of Huggies toddlers during periods with no ad feature or in-store display.
f. The retailer never promotes both sizes of Huggies at the same time, and all promotions, including price reduction without feature or display, are one week long. At the end of the week, regular price is restored and the retailer sells any remainder of the promotional purchase at regular price. Allocation to ad only, display only, ad and display events, and price reduction only events is the same for both the medium and toddler sizes. If the event is in-store display only, no reduction in shelf price is used. If the event is ad only, or an ad and display combination, it is at 1-cent per diaper discount from regular shelf price.

Question 3   Use linear interpolation between the tabled values of the price and promotion responses in Figure 4-1 and Figure 4-2. Evaluate the impact of the promotional program on:
a. Huggies medium volume sales
b. Huggies toddler volume sales
c. Medium and toddler combined volume sales

Question 4   Using the incremental volume estimated in Question 1, estimate the cost to the manufacturer of Huggies per incremental unit obtained through promotion. Estimate this by size and type of retail sales promotion, both on an individual event basis and summarized across the promotional program for each size.

Question 5   Suppose that an audit of retail store performance on Huggies promotional offers indicates that of the 40 percent of accepted offers that do not receive feature or display support, there is a 50-50 split between complete pass-through of the allowance by reduced price and maintaining regular shelf price with no pass-through of the allowance. Redo Questions 3 and 4 with this assumption.

Question 6   Suppose Huggies management wishes to improve retailer support via feature ad and/or in-store display. Since it is difficult to audit stores for shelf price reduction, management is considering the use of a feature audit service to assure that Huggies has been featured before the promotional allowance is given. Management's assessment of the impact of this change in promotional requirements is that of the 40 percent of accepted offers that do not receive feature or display, 3 out of 4 would refuse the promotional offer, and 1 out of 4 would run feature only with complete pass-through of promotional allowance. Those accounts that currently give feature only or feature and display support would not alter their behavior. Of the accounts that currently give display only support, half would refuse the offer, and half would feature with no pass-through of the promotional allowance. There would be no change in the promotion schedule given in Assumption e (Question 2). Compare the estimated sales volumes and promotional costs of this program to those estimates generated in Question 5.

Question 7   Suppose that the pass-through of non-supported offers is as estimated in Question 5. The response to a requirement for feature support is as estimated in Question 6, and the current distribution of retail support by feature or display is as shown in the case background. Management asks you to design an improved promotion for the combined medium and toddler Huggies. They are not willing to provide variable cost information, but do indicate that retailers take the same percentage mark-up on both sizes, and that the variable costs as a percent of manufacturer list price are the same for both sizes. Spending to stimulate retail sales promotion is not considered as part of variable cost.

You are free to alter the number of events per year for each size subject to the following limitations:
a. Each size must have at least one promotional offer per year with at least 1 cent discount from manufacturer list per diaper.
b. A size can have a maximum of nine events per year.
c. The retailer must be allowed to purchase at discount an amount equal to at least two weeks regular sales if an offer on a size is accepted.
d. There is no inexpensive method of auditing accounts for in-store display activity, so performance for a feature and display combination will yield the same distribution of event types as will a requirement for proof of featuring.

Management requests that you prepare proposed programs and volume estimates for three levels of promotional budget:
a. The current level implied by the case background
b. A budget of 125 percent of the current level
c. A budget of 75 percent of the current level

Case: Fabric Softener

In 1983, Lever Brothers introduced Snuggle, a liquid fabric softener. Total fabric softener products include both liquid forms (about 60 percent), and drier-added fabric softener (about 40 percent).

Background   Snuggle was priced much lower than most competing liquids, and the brand's advertising has a strong economy theme.

Brand shares before and after the Snuggle introduction are shown in Table 4-6.

The introduction of Snuggle more than doubled Lever Brothers share of this market, and was achieved with little cannibalization of their existing

Table 4-6

LIQUID FABRIC SOFTENER MANUFACTURER/BRAND	BRAND SHARES PRE AND POST SNUGGLE INTRODUCTION 1982 SHARE	1983 SHARE
Lever Brothers	10.8	25.6
Final Touch	10.8	11.7
Snuggle	N/A	13.9
Procter & Gamble	48.9	40.0
Downy	48.9	40.0
All Other	40.3	34.4

product. One of the regional rollouts of Snuggle occurred in a market where the vast majority of grocery sales were monitored by scanners, and where the individual purchasing behavior of over 2,000 households was constantly monitored.

In the brand's first 23 weeks on the market, 21.1 percent of all households in the sample had purchased Snuggle at least once. That represented about half of all fabric softener buyers during that time period. Further, after 23 weeks, 46.3 percent of all Snuggle triers had made at least one repeat purchase. One of the reasons for reaching this level of trial was the level of retail dealing achieved by Snuggle.

During the introductory period, 55 percent of Snuggle volume was moved with some combination of retail support, including ad feature, in-store display, price reduction, and store coupon. The primary vehicle was display, with 46 percent of Snuggle volume moved from in-store display. Ads and displays were often at regular price, with only 28 percent of volume moved with shelf price reduction. When reductions occurred, the average percent price reduction was 38 percent. Both retail store coupons and manufacturer coupons were used extensively, with 32 percent of Snuggle volume purchased with coupon discounts.

For comparison, Downy moved 35 percent of its volume with trade deals. About 24 percent of Downy volume was moved from in-store display. Shelf price reduction was in effect on 16 percent of Downy sales, and the average percent reduction was 18 percent. Only 8 percent of Downy volume was purchased with coupon discounts. Table 4-7 shows a selection of the Snuggle trial curve and the associated dealing levels.

To provide a detailed assessment of the sources of Snuggle volume, a direct comparison of the purchase mix among triers after trial versus the same

Table 4-7
SNUGGLE DEALING LEVELS

WEEK SINCE INTRODUCTION	CUMULATIVE PERCENT OF CATEGORY BUYERS BUYING SNUGGLE	PERCENT SNUGGLE VOLUME DURING WEEK WITH TRADE DEAL
8	8.2	1.5
9	11.8	2.3
10	15.4	1.0
11	24.3	69.8
12	29.3	40.6

Table 4-8
SNUGGLE SOURCE OF VOLUME ANALYSIS

SOURCE	PERCENT OF SNUGGLE VOLUME	
From Other Liquids	45.6	
Final Touch		5.0
Downy		25.9
All Other Liquids		14.7
From Drier Type	9.5	
Increased Category Consumption	43.1	
Consumption increase from existing fabric softener users		26.5
New fabric softener buyers		16.6

households' purchase mix prior to Snuggle trial was conducted on a household by household basis. These results were summed across households to provide a composite picture. This analysis of the buying patterns of households which tried Snuggle indicated that Snuggle achieved its volume from the sources shown in Table 4-8.

Advertising in the introductory campaign was monitored as well. In the market being considered, 1,000 households were equipped with television meters that recorded the channel being viewed at 5-second intervals. All television broadcast activity in the marketplace was monitored for th exact time that each program and advertisement started and stopped. By matching the broadcast data and viewing data, individual households can be classified with respect to program viewership, and number of exposures they have had to any particular brand's advertising.

In the first six months on the market, Snuggle delivered 1,640 gross rating points, representing 97.9 percent reach with an average frequency of 16.7. Of the total delivery, 58 percent went to households that did not buy either liquid or drier type fabric softeners during the six-month period.

Table 4-9 shows the relationship of promotion and liquid fabric softeners in two stores. Use these tables to answer the following questions.

Table 4-9
LIQUID FABRIC SOFTENER SALES

---STORE=A---

TOTAL CATEGORY			FINAL TOUCH			SNUGGLE		
WEEK	VOLUME	DOLLARS	VOLUME	PRICE	PROMO	VOLUME	PRICE	PROMO
1	87.681	144.37	11.0	2.04		.	.	.
2	141.858	224.94	7.1	2.28		.	.	.
3	103.181	164.98	5.5	2.28		.	.	.
4	65.883	107.28	7.6	2.30		.	.	.
5	84.780	132.17	8.1	2.41		.	.	.
6	90.695	133.70	2.0	2.33		.	.	.

Table 4-9 (CONTINUED)
LIQUID FABRIC SOFTENER SALES
--STORE=A--

TOTAL CATEGORY			FINAL TOUCH			SNUGGLE		
WEEK	VOLUME	DOLLARS	VOLUME	PRICE	PROMO	VOLUME	PRICE	PROMO
7	137.188	203.11	5.6	2.44	.	.	.	.
8	106.925	167.06	7.6	2.42	.	.	.	.
9	99.379	158.11	5.5	2.43	.	.	.	.
10	83.532	128.20	9.0	2.20	.	.	.	.
11	95.174	159.26	7.6	2.37	.	.	.	.
12	144.702	215.54	3.1	2.65	.	.	.	.
13	164.184	214.68	3.1	2.65	.	.	.	.
14	102.255	157.74	7.1	2.42	.	.	.	.
15	57.184	87.40	6.1	2.47	.	.	.	.
16	103.447	159.49	9.1	2.69	.	.	.	.
17	118.713	175.27	3.5	2.72	.	.	.	.
18	131.199	193.46	4.1	2.75	.	.	.	.
19	84.879	126.17	3.0	2.69	.	.	.	.
20	152.362	227.89	6.1	2.56	.	.	.	.
21	93.762	152.51	12.6	2.56	.	.	.	.
22	79.514	109.64	2.5	2.02		19.0	1.14	.
23	145.351	186.94	5.5	2.15		80.0	1.13	D
24	186.220	196.76	6.0	1.54		119.5	0.90	D
25	249.940	254.33	3.6	1.76		116.9	0.94	D
26	175.940	183.38	5.5	1.57		111.1	0.93	D
27	163.496	161.69	2.0	1.54		52.9	0.94	
28	383.954	331.74	1.5	1.58		263.4	0.85	FD
29	280.659	243.91	1.0	1.54		104.1	0.89	D
30	231.766	188.34	2.0	1.60		136.9	0.77	
31	133.681	125.37	5.1	1.59		99.0	0.81	
32	157.940	140.41	3.5	2.15		128.9	0.78	D
33	137.358	136.16	1.5	1.36		93.9	0.84	
34	123.376	123.13	1.0	1.70		85.6	0.83	
35	105.046	114.50	0.5	2.04		52.8	0.93	
36	92.429	113.91	3.5	1.90		50.5	1.15	
37	96.425	115.94	4.0	2.28		40.8	0.97	
38	140.723	159.30	3.0	2.25		76.1	1.07	
39	146.199	168.87	2.0	1.54		64.3	1.07	
40	102.638	113.41	2.0	2.32		62.5	1.01	
41	102.394	122.05	2.5	1.81		51.2	1.09	
42	102.723	134.06	1.0	1.73		39.4	1.25	
43	95.759	115.00	2.0	1.73		63.8	1.12	D
44	123.082	132.23	0.5	2.14		78.9	0.95	D
45	150.113	142.51	0.0	.		44.3	0.95	
46	316.638	245.87	1.0	1.61		247.3	0.69	
47	169.245	157.78	1.5	1.79		132.6	0.84	D
48	119.461	116.47	3.0	1.61		80.4	0.90	D
49	97.567	102.32	1.0	2.48		51.0	0.90	
50	229.830	167.62	2.0	1.88		27.1	0.96	
51	211.057	176.53	1.0	1.61		34.8	1.01	
52	183.397	156.05	3.0	1.79		16.6	0.96	

Table 4-9 (CONTINUED)

--STORE=A--

TOTAL CATEGORY			DOWNY			ALL OTHER LIQUID FAB SFNR		
WEEK	VOLUME	DOLLARS	VOLUME	PRICE	PROMO	VOLUME	PRICE	PROMO
1	87.681	144.37	63.2	1.71	D	13.5	1.02	
2	141.858	224.94	106.2	1.61	D	28.6	1.31	
3	103.181	164.98	81.6	1.61		16.1	1.33	
4	65.883	107.28	39.2	1.67		19.1	1.28	
5	84.780	132.17	55.7	1.64		21.0	1.01	
6	90.695	133.70	67.7	1.59		21.0	1.01	
7	137.188	203.11	107.6	1.53	D	23.9	1.05	
8	106.925	167.06	73.9	1.65		25.4	1.04	
9	99.379	158.11	77.4	1.64		16.5	1.09	
10	83.532	128.20	50.6	1.67		23.9	1.00	
11	95.174	159.36	76.0	1.64		11.6	1.46	
12	144.702	215.54	118.6	1.53	D	23.0	1.15	
13	164.184	214.68	147.7	1.31	F	13.5	0.94	
14	102.255	157.74	75.2	1.55		20.0	1.21	
15	57.184	87.40	37.7	1.56		13.5	1.02	
16	103.447	159.49	75.8	1.50		18.5	1.14	
17	118.713	175.27	99.6	1.48	D	15.5	1.16	
18	131.199	193.46	108.6	1.48	D	18.5	1.17	
19	84.879	126.17	68.4	1.52		13.5	1.05	
20	152.362	227.89	128.3	1.51	D	18.0	1.06	
21	93.762	152.51	66.2	1.58		15.0	1.06	
22	79.514	109.64	41.5	1.58		16.5	1.05	
23	145.351	186.94	46.7	1.44		13.1	1.35	
24	186.220	196.76	46.7	1.36		14.0	1.14	
25	249.940	254.33	109.4	1.05		20.0	1.16	
26	175.940	183.38	54.2	1.17		5.0	1.65	
27	163.496	161.69	101.1	1.00	D	7.5	0.99	
28	383.954	331.74	114.5	0.88	D	4.5	0.94	
29	280.659	243.91	169.9	0.82	D	5.6	1.82	
30	231.766	188.34	89.9	0.85		3.0	1.07	
31	133.681	125.37	24.0	1.12		5.6	1.89	
32	157.940	140.41	24.0	1.30		1.5	0.94	
33	137.358	136.16	32.3	1.33		9.5	1.32	
34	123.376	123.13	30.2	1.34		6.5	1.49	
35	105.046	114.50	39.8	1.32		12.0	1.00	
36	92.429	113.91	32.4	1.34		6.0	0.94	
37	96.425	115.94	39.1	1.33		12.5	1.23	
38	140.723	159.30	49.6	1.19		12.0	1.00	
39	146.199	168.87	68.3	1.17		11.6	1.49	
40	102.638	113.41	27.1	1.14		11.0	1.33	
41	102.394	122.05	41.2	1.32		7.5	0.95	
42	102.723	134.06	52.8	1.33		9.5	1.32	
43	95.759	115.00	23.4	1.35		6.5	1.35	
44	123.082	132.23	36.2	1.35		7.5	1.00	
45	150.113	142.51	99.8	0.94	FD	6.0	1.08	
46	316.638	245.87	53.4	1.12		15.0	0.97	

Table 4-9 (CONTINUED)

---STORE=A---

TOTAL CATEGORY			DOWNY			ALL OTHER LIQUID FAB SFNR		
WEEK	VOLUME	DOLLARS	VOLUME	PRICE	PROMO	VOLUME	PRICE	PROMO
47	169.245	157.78	30.1	1.19		5.0	1.58	
48	119.461	116.47	27.1	1.10		9.0	1.06	
49	97.567	102.32	40.0	1.08		5.6	1.92	
50	229.830	167.62	199.2	0.69	FD	1.5	0.97	
51	211.057	176.53	142.3	0.82	D	32.9	0.68	FD
52	183.397	156.05	143.8	0.84	D	20.0	0.72	D

---STORE=B---

TOTAL CATEGORY			FINAL TOUCH			SNUGGLE		
WEEK	VOLUME	DOLLARS	VOLUME	PRICE	PROMO	VOLUME	PRICE	PROMO
1	287.950	407.150	16.0	2.50		.	.	.
2	336.184	469.430	19.0	2.34		.	.	.
3	316.177	453.630	20.5	2.24		.	.	.
4	303.723	447.760	14.5	2.27		.	.	.
5	233.652	351.970	12.5	2.55		.	.	.
6	284.191	422.960	19.5	2.55		.	.	.
7	318.617	448.160	13.0	2.54		.	.	.
8	301.340	447.540	24.5	2.21		.	.	.
9	287.149	446.610	39.9	2.05		.	.	.
10	257.808	373.490	15.5	2.55		.	.	.
11	303.652	439.340	23.0	2.44		.	.	.
12	263.901	389.810	19.0	2.28		.	.	.
13	276.546	375.710	16.0	2.25		.	.	.
14	238.922	342.090	25.0	2.22		.	.	.
15	263.347	361.530	17.5	2.19		.	.	.
16	266.071	357.800	21.0	2.23		.	.	.
17	226.964	315.160	15.5	2.20		.	.	.
18	272.511	404.140	29.5	2.25		.	.	.
19	256.773	371.770	29.5	2.25		.	.	.
20	412.205	591.540	37.5	2.22		.	.	.
21	288.730	388.680	18.0	2.15		.	.	.
22	284.929	383.630	19.0	2.28		.	.	.
23	264.383	333.700	22.5	2.09		.	.	.
24	307.298	371.590	21.5	2.06		34.7	1.11	
25	375.454	424.150	10.0	1.98		36.9	1.11	
26	411.936	464.290	15.0	2.06		178.6	0.98	
27	433.631	472.650	7.0	2.23		25.7	0.98	D
28	446.936	482.819	6.5	2.23		293.7	0.98	D
29	324.496	363.180	4.0	2.23		130.2	1.12	
30	287.241	345.300	16.5	2.23		105.4	1.11	
31	526.858	459.900	3.5	2.23		407.1	0.81	D
32	378.120	356.810	4.0	2.24		239.3	0.82	D
33	449.837	400.570	0.0	.		304.7	0.81	D
34	486.135	441.800	5.0	2.24		342.9	0.82	D

Table 4-9 (CONTINUED)

---STORE=B--

TOTAL CATEGORY			FINAL TOUCH			SNUGGLE		
WEEK	VOLUME	DOLLARS	VOLUME	PRICE	PROMO	VOLUME	PRICE	PROMO
35	268.553	267.890	6.5	2.15		133.7	0.87	
36	245.957	270.920	8.0	2.12		96.3	0.92	
37	270.447	292.130	5.5	2.07		106.9	0.95	
38	351.574	389.320	14.0	2.03		140.0	0.93	
39	316.057	332.730	13.0	1.89		112.0	0.90	
40	264.191	292.670	8.0	1.65		98.6	0.88	
41	221.035	231.050	9.0	1.70		81.3	0.89	
42	263.624	281.570	9.0	1.79		106.7	0.89	
43	223.709	242.040	12.0	1.77		92.7	0.92	
44	228.936	249.080	5.0	1.54		91.9	0.92	
45	229.284	260.810	37.0	1.54		76.1	0.95	
46	298.780	356.760	58.0	1.54	D	65.5	0.97	
47	343.638	341.270	16.5	1.60		210.4	0.87	D
48	359.354	347.340	7.5	1.67		232.8	0.86	D
49	276.028	281.010	8.5	1.66		162.6	0.87	D
50	306.525	308.180	12.5	1.62		173.0	0.86	D
51	274.156	325.300	61.0	1.54	D	70.8	1.09	
52	228.915	286.060	49.5	1.56	D	83.6	1.10	

---STORE=B--

TOTAL CATEGORY			DOWNY			ALL OTHER LIQUID FAB SFNR		
WEEK	VOLUME	DOLLARS	VOLUME	PRICE	PROMO	VOLUME	PRICE	PROMO
1	287.950	407.150	185.0	1.56		87.0	0.89	
2	336.184	469.430	210.6	1.56		106.6	0.90	
3	316.177	453.630	203.1	1.56		92.6	0.97	
4	303.723	447.760	205.3	1.56		84.0	1.13	
5	233.652	351.970	146.2	1.57		75.0	1.20	
6	284.191	422.960	181.5	1.57		83.2	1.07	
7	318.617	448.160	192.1	1.57		113.5	1.00	
8	301.340	447.540	190.5	1.57		86.4	1.10	
9	287.149	446.610	168.5	1.56		78.7	1.28	
10	257.808	373.490	153.1	1.58		89.2	1.04	
11	303.652	439.340	184.5	1.57		96.1	0.97	
12	263.901	389.810	176.8	1.57		68.1	1.02	
13	276.546	375.710	176.0	1.47		84.5	0.96	
14	238.922	342.090	154.8	1.44		59.1	1.09	
15	263.347	361.530	162.6	1.44		83.2	1.08	
16	266.071	357.800	152.9	1.42		92.2	1.02	
17	226.964	315.160	145.3	1.48		66.2	1.00	
18	272.511	404.140	159.8	1.54		83.2	1.10	
19	256.773	371.770	144.1	1.49		83.2	1.10	
20	412.205	591.540	285.0	1.45		89.8	1.05	
21	288.730	388.680	198.0	1.37		72.8	1.09	
22	284.929	383.630	200.3	1.37		65.7	1.00	
23	264.383	333.700	167.1	1.20		74.8	1.16	

Table 4-9 (CONTINUED)
---STORE=B---

| TOTAL CATEGORY | | | DOWNY | | | ALL OTHER LIQUID FAB SFNR | | |
WEEK	VOLUME	DOLLARS	VOLUME	PRICE	PROMO	VOLUME	PRICE	PROMO
24	307.298	371.590	175.0	1.19		76.1	1.05	
25	375.454	424.150	220.1	1.19		108.5	0.93	
26	411.936	464.290	181.2	1.19		37.2	1.14	
27	433.631	472.650	126.1	1.19		48.8	1.26	
28	446.936	482.819	105.2	1.19		41.5	1.37	
29	324.496	363.180	140.4	1.18		49.9	0.86	
30	287.241	345.300	112.1	1.19		53.3	1.10	
31	526.858	459.900	75.9	1.19		40.4	0.83	
32	378.120	356.810	98.4	1.21		36.5	0.88	
33	449.837	400.570	105.1	1.12		40.0	0.93	
34	486.135	441.800	88.7	1.18		49.6	0.92	
35	268.553	267.890	86.5	1.19		41.9	0.84	
36	245.957	270.920	114.0	1.18		27.7	1.09	
37	270.447	292.130	121.0	1.19		37.0	0.95	
38	351.574	389.320	144.2	1.19		53.3	1.11	
39	316.057	332.730	127.1	1.19		64.0	0.89	
40	264.191	292.670	120.2	1.19		37.4	1.34	
41	221.035	231.050	102.3	1.19		28.4	0.76	
42	263.624	281.570	111.3	1.19		36.7	1.06	
43	223.709	242.040	90.9	1.19		28.1	1.00	
44	228.936	249.080	74.4	1.19		57.6	1.19	D
45	229.284	260.810	80.6	1.19		35.5	1.01	D
46	298.780	356.760	126.1	1.18		49.2	1.12	D
47	343.638	341.270	82.7	1.19		34.0	0.98	D
48	359.354	347.340	84.1	1.18		35.0	1.00	D
49	276.028	281.010	69.2	1.19		35.7	1.22	
50	306.525	308.180	92.4	1.18		28.6	1.02	
51	274.156	325.300	104.4	1.18		38.0	0.81	
52	228.915	286.060	65.5	1.19		30.3	1.27	

Question 1 Discuss the impact of trade dealing on the trial rate of Snuggle.

Question 2 Review the differences in the price and promotion strategies of Final Touch, Downy, and Snuggle in Store A and Store B. What defensive strategy would you recommend for Downy?

Question 3 Estimate the response to price discounts and promotional activity for Final Touch, Downy, and Snuggle. For Downy, estimate how many weeks of a price reduction of 20 cents without feature or display activity would be required to generate the same incremental volume for Downy as one week of in-store display with 20 cent price reduction.

Question 4 Store B is planning to put up a display on Downy in Week 53 at a price of 99¢. The manager and analysts for Store B only have access to their own store sales history, and must make an estimate of probable Downy sales on this event in order to order enough product to avoid out-of-stocks. Using only the data from Store B, what is your best estimate of the probable sales of Downy on this event? How much product would you want to have available to reduce the chances of running out of stock to only about 1 in 20?

**Question 5
(Term Project)**   Collect information on the current competitive conditions that exist in the fabric softener market in your area. Visit several grocery stores, and note the current shelf space allocations to Downy, Final Touch, Snuggle, and other liquid fabric softeners. Note the price relations now existing, and monitor store pricing and promotional activity over a period of four to six weeks. Locate product reviews in consumer magazines that indicate strengths and weaknesses that might exist among the various products. Prepare a report summarizing your findings.

5 Retailer Strategies

Retailers can effectively use sales promotion themselves apart from any strategies employed by manufacturers. In fact, almost any of the same techniques can be applied with similar results. The retailer should, however, analyze its sales promotion programs in much the same way—from a financial perspective.

Pricing, Margin, and Profits

The retailer, like the manufacturer, must always consider the impact a sales promotion program will have on the profitability of the firm. A retailer must also be aware that there is a fundamental relationship between the selling price of products and the sales volume of those products. The retailer has the advantage over the manufacturer in being able to directly estimate this relationship without having to rely on intervening organizations. In other words, the retailer doesn't need to go through other distributors like the manufacturer does to reach the final customer.

The retailer, like the manufacturer, should also obtain weekly or daily sales data by outlet and estimate the appropriate demand curve. If the retailer already collects scanner data and has the necessary computing power, it is certainly possible that he could perform all the analysis internally. The retailer could also use an external research organization just as the manufacturer could.

The retailer should analyze a product in terms of its contributions to margin, to selling expenses, and to profit. Ideally, the retailer could perform such an analysis for every product that is sold in the store. The problem, of course, is that this would require thousands of analyses, making it somewhat impractical for most retailers.

A partial solution would be to select either high volume products or products that are deemed especially important to the retail outlet for whatever reason. A product may have a history of building store traffic, or it might have special seasonal significance, or maybe it would be especially attractive because of special allowances and offers made by the manufacturer. Despite the difficulties, the retailer should carefully examine the profitablity of a given promotion in the same way as should the manufacturer.

Trade Promotion

A major consideration for any retailer should be trade promotions from manufacturers. Trade promotions come in several forms, including the familiar trade allowance or trade deal, and even interest promotions, such as contests and sweepstakes, for the trade. Normally trade promotion is supported by a manufacturer with advertising, in-store displays and related material, and sometimes additional consumer promotion. Cooperative advetising programs may be part of the package offered by the manufacturer as well.

All of the offers made by the manufacturer can potentially stretch the retailer's promotional budget and increase this profit. The trade allowance usually means a short-term reduction in price from the manufacturer, which immediately translates to reduced cost of goods for the retailer. Other advertising and promotional support from the manufacturer can substantially reduce the retailer's promotional expenses. The cost to the retailer is giving that manufacturer special advantage within the store and the potential of shifting sales volume from high profit items to lower profit items.

The retailer must carefully weigh the decision to take advantage of any manufacturer's offers, especially since there are likely to be many such offers. The retailer must consider each offer in light of alternative promotion offers, the customer that the retailer currently serves or wishes to attract, the likely profit directly generated by the promotion, and possible cannibalization effects.

Competitive Stores

A retail store must view competitive stores in almost the same way that a manufacturer must view competing product brands. The retailer gives very special attention to the kind of customers it currently enjoys and considers what kind of customer a sales promotion program is likely to attract.

Source of Store Business

The same ways of describing purchasers of a particular brand can be used to describe shoppers at a particular store. The same basic variables, including brand loyalty, deal proneness, and product usage can all be adapted to the individual store. Instead of brand loyalty, the concept becomes store loyalty within the type of store within a geographical location. Product usage can be easily translated into store category usage.

A 1984 study by IRI has found that supermarkets, for example, can be readily grouped according to their sales volume. The highest group, that is, the group with the highest average weekly sales volume, tends to have the greatest proportion of loyal customers. In fact, loyal shoppers account for about one-fifth of the store's shoppers, but these loyal shoppers account for nearly two-fifths of the store's sales volume. While loyal shoppers may be very important to a store, almost all shoppers at least visit other stores during a 12-week time period. Just less than one out of ten shoppers visits only one store in this period. Approximately half visit three or four stores, and about one-fourth visit five or more stores. Thus a store's pricing and promotional practices will probably be subjected to comparison with the practices of competing stores.

Consumer deal proneness is an extremely important variable as well. As might be expected, IRI has found a strong and increasing relation between the importance of promotion to a consumer and the increase in number of stores visited.

While these numbers are interesting in themselves, they are averages. Some stores would enjoy business from shoppers who tend to be more loyal, and other stores might receive considerably more business from shoppers who visit many stores and are very sensitive to promotion. It is important that the retailer understand the nature of the business it has. One key factor is the physical location of competing stores. An isolated store is less sensitive to the advertised prices of competing retailers than a store located physically close to one or more competitors.

Cherry Picking

As the volume of promotion has increased, more consumers are able to buy more products that take advantage of some type of promotion more often. This has created a relatively new shopper segment described by the term *cherry picking*. A shopper who cherry picks is one who almost always buys products that are being sold with some type of promotional offer. This is a phenomenon that is an important side effect of the growing volume of sales promotion.

Store Switching

A shopper might tend to be loyal to a particular store, just as to a particular brand, or may tend to frequently switch stores. In the first case, the shopper might be categorized as being store loyal and in the latter case categorized as being a store switcher. The store can use this consumer characteristic in the same way as a manufacturer can use brand switching. The physical proximity of competitors will be an important determinant of store loyalty.

Store Coupons and Double Couponing

Coupons are a common form of sales promotion, making them a very competitive form. Coupon clutter has become a major concern today because of the tremendous number of coupons distributed to consumers. The number of coupons distributed has increased in recent years, making them an increasingly popular technique. As the popularity increases, there is more opportunity for stores to take advantage of them.

The store has very little control over the coupons that are issued by the manufacturer. The manufacturer can place the coupons on and in the package, or distribute them through the media. The only work left for the store is to redeem them.

In order for the store itself to take advantage of opportunities that coupons represent, it must offer its own coupons or take special advantage of the manufacturer coupons and offer a "double" or "triple" coupon. A retail or *store coupon*, that is, a coupon offered by a store and redeemable by that store, may or may not be in response to a trade allowance or other special incentive provided to the retailer by a manufacturer. The store, interested in generating store traffic, might pick any single product or combination of products that would provide the greatest advantage. Trade coupons, or store coupons, are then entirely the responsibility of the store management.

Knowing that the manufacturer coupons are available to consumers in abundant supply, and that the coupons may be redeemed at virtually any supermarket in the area, induces some stores to offer special additional incentives to coupon holders. The additional incentive is an offer such as a *double coupon*, that is, giving the consumer twice the face value of the manufacturer coupon. If a coupon offer is 10 cents off, then the store would offer 20 cents. The store, of course, would need to absorb the additional 10 cents.

Some stores offer other versions of double couponing, perhaps even triple couponing. Some stores may even offer to redeem competing store or trade coupons. The important consideration, regardless of the offer, is the profit that the promotional program provides the store. The store should be guided by the same underlying principles as the manufacturer. One particularly effective usage is the practice of giving double or triple coupon value only during selected hours of operation, such as Tuesday only, or 11 p.m. to 6 a.m. Such practices can balance labor requirements or checkout and restocking.

Private Brands and Generic Brands

Larger store chains or members of wholesale groups often are able to offer private brands and generic brands. Private brands are brands that are owned by the retailer or wholesaler rather than the manufacturer. Generic brands are products offered with no brand identification at all. Both private brands and generic brands are usually offered to consumers at normal prices lower than the manufacturer brands.

Part of the reason the private and generic brands have lower prices is that they do not require the same margin from the manufacturer as do the manufacturer's own brands because the selling expenses are considerably lower. The manufacturer does not have the same selling, advertising, and promotion expenses. This means, however, that the retailer does not have the same advertising and sales promotion support for the private and generic brands that is available for the manufacturer's brand. The store itself must bear all of the selling expense associated with the private brand. Any sales promotion program is entirely at the expense of the store.

Manufacturers who supply private and generic brands to the trade may also be packaging a lower quality product, keeping the highest quality product for their own brand. This is especially convenient for food packagers that are always faced with a differing quality in the raw material they are able to obtain. Products that may have a less desirable color, for example, would be more likely to be packaged as a private or generic brand.

Private and generic brands shift all of the advertising and promotional responsibility to the retailer. Presumably the private and generic brands generate a greater margin for the store, but may also incur greater selling expenses.

Continuity Promotions

Not only are retailers interested in generating store traffic with promotional programs, but they are also interested in promoting store loyalty. One method of providing an incentive for store loyalty is the continuity promotion. Continuity promotions are typified by trading stamp programs and store premium programs. Store premium programs are normally designed so that one piece of a set, such as a set of books or dishes, can be purchased each week.

There are several problems with continuity programs. First is that they normally take a long time to run. A trading stamp program, for example, must run for several years. It is difficult to change or stop, thus obligating the store for a long period of time to the promotional program. Another problem with continuity programs is that the offer may not appeal to all consumers, or even to a very large proportion of consumers. Books, for example, might appeal only to a very small segment. Also, consumers usually want immediate gratification, and may not want to wait over an extended period of time to complete the set. Another problem is that continuity promotions do not always tie in well with other promotions and displays. Continuity promotions represent a relatively small proportion of the promotional programs, but represent a viable alternative.

Retailer Decisions

When the retailer receives a promotional program from a manufacturer, the retailer is faced with several decisions. The promotional program offered by a manufacturer probably includes a trade allowance, consumer promotions such as coupons, consumer advertising support, and in-store display material. It must also be remembered that the retailer receives many promotional offers from manufacturers as part of the normal course of doing business. Of course, promotional programs would be available from competing manufacturers in the same product category. It is probably also true that the typical retailer could not possible use all of the promotional material provided by all of the manufacturers. The retailer must be somewhat selective in the promotional programs used and must make some decisions.

Use the Display

Probably one of the resources that is in shortest supply for most retailers is display space. Space on shelves, at the end of aisles, and in other locations in the store is usually very limited. In-store point-of-purchase displays are very frequently supplied by manufacturers to support both consumer advertising and promotional programs. The problem for the retailer is, of course, which displays to use.

The retailer may also want to use displays that are not provided by the manufacturers, but rather use those developed by the retailer, or not use any display at all. To make the best decision, the retailer must understand the effect of the display on sales of the product.

Change the Regular Price

When a product is sold to the retailer with a trade allowance, the retailer must decide whether or not to pass along the price reduction to the consumer. The argument for not lowering the regular price would be that the margin would increase, thereby increasing the profitability. The argument for lowering the price might be that the volume would increase, thereby increasing the profitability. Accurate assessment of price and volume relations is required to make this decision. Another consideration must also be the competitive environment that the store is in, which may mean that lowering the price would have impact on store traffic.

Additional Price Reduction

A store, knowing that the competing retailers in the market area may also be receiving the same trade allowance or other special price promotion from the manufacturer, may want to increase the incentive by providing an additional price reduction. An additional price reduction not only provides the retailer with a competitive edge over other retailers, but it also takes advantages of the advertising and promotion that the manufacturer already has in place. Rather than trying to overcome or to compete with the manufacturer's efforts in the very crowded and cluttered media and promotional environment, the retailer can reinforce the manufacturer's program and probably reap substantially greater benefit.

Additional Promotions   In the same way that a retailer can take advantage of a special price by increasing the offer, the retailer can provide additional promotion to support the manufacturer's effort. The retailer can also feature the promotion in its own advertising, emphasizing the special price or other aspects of a promotion. Not only does using additional promotion provide the opportunity to increase the impact of the program, but it may also provide the retailer with the opportunity to take advantage of cooperative advertising programs the manufacturer may have.

The criterion the retailer should use for these decisions should be the same as the manufacturer: profit. The retailer must be able to perform the same type of analysis as the manufacturer.

Retailer Buying Decisions

When a trade allowance or other special price offer is made by the manufacturer, the retailer must make the decision whether or not to buy. Some of the considerations here involve much more than promotion, and for more discussion a book dealing with retail inventory management should be consulted.

Promotion Buying   Any time a special price offer is made by a manufacturer, there is a temptation to buy because the cost of goods is reduced. The question, of course, is how much, if any, of the product should be purchased at the promotional price.

A major consideration for the retailer should be what volume can be sold to the consumer at what price. Certainly if the retailer can sell additional volume of the product at a special price and make additional profit, then the retailer should purchase the appropriate volume of the product. It is of course critical that the retailer be able to estimate the volume it can sell at various price levels. Otherwise the decision becomes guesswork.

A store that overbuys a product at a special promotional price is in a position of having to lower the price beyond the point of generating profit, and in fact may actually incur loss. A store that has too much inventory must pay carrying costs for that inventory. The other side of the problem is that too little inventory may result in an out-of-stock situation, which loses the opportunity to make a sale and may substantially reduce the long-term image of the store. Out-of-stock on a promotional item may anger customers and cause loss of goodwill.

Forward Buying   Promotional programs offered by manufacturers often not only provide the retailer an opportunity to buy a product at a special price, but to have the product delivered at a time in the future different from normal delivery. This provides the manufacturer with more stability in the business and may provide operating cash. From the point of view of the retailer, the product is available at a lower price, with a longer planning time horizon to prepare promotional and advertising programs. All of the same principles apply to this situation as they do to all of the other promotional decisions faced by the retailer.

Goodwill and Carryover

The long-term image of the store is a very important consideration for the retailer. Taking advantage of special promotional offers from manufacturers should be seriously considered. The retailer must carefully evaluate its source of business and make sure that the promotional programs it takes advantage of do not seriously damage the store's image. For example, a store can easily become known as a store that doesn't have a good selection and only sells items that no one really wants. The long-term impact of selling heavily promoted items might be damaging to the image of the store and to the goodwill that store may have established. However, an "everyday low price" may be a strong positive for the store.

Manufacturer and Retailer Interactive Strategies

Throughout this book, there have been repeated examples of manufacturer sales promotion programs that have been successful in generating profit. There have also been examples of sales promotion programs that have been successful for retailers. The most effective strategies, however, are those where the efforts of the manufacturer and the retailer work together.

When the manufacturer and retailer strategies supplement and reinforce each other, the effect is almost always considerably better than the two strategies would have been if they were not carefully coordinated. The advertising and sales promotion done by the manufacturer is always considerably more effective when it is reinforced by the advertising and sales promotion done by the retailer, and vice versa. Strategies that interact always do a much better job of breaking through the clutter and reaching the consumer.

A retailer must carefully weigh the advantages of supporting a manufacturer's program with the additional impact against the competitive pressures of other retailers. A retailer may want to avoid participating in a program that may be more effective overall, but may weaken the relative competitive position among other retailers.

Pizza company offers to redeem any competitor's coupon.

To build store traffic, Cub Stores offers free eggs (left). Eagle features the products of a specific manufacturer, Procter & Gamble, in its ROP ad (below left). Dominick's uses a sweepstakes to promote loyalty to its chain of stores (below).

Jewel offers retailer deep discount coupons with a minimum purchase requirement (right). Jewel's offer of fine china is a continuity retailer promotion (below). And Jewel also features its private label brands in an ROP newspaper ad (below right).

ROP newspaper ad for Family Drug Center is an example of a retailer newspaper page.

ROP ad for Aldi shows how retailers use newspaper ads to feature "everyday low prices."

Case: Frozen Waffles

The examination of store sales indicates that there is often a substantial increase in sales volume associated with trade deal activity. The sources of the volume increase are usually difficult to determine from store sales data. Some of the possible sources of sales increases are:

- Attracting new category triers
- Switching buyers out of other brands
- Stimulating increased consumption by buyers
- Encouraging stockpiling by brand buyers who purchase extra items and then have longer than average times to the next purchase as they use up the excess
- Encouraging purchases by switchers, who have a set of several brands that are acceptable and purchase the cheapest item in the set at the time of the purchase
- Generating purchases by deal-prone buyers who usually buy only with trade deals or manufacturer coupons
- Drawing sales from other area stores

These possibilities are not mutually exclusive. Switchers, for example, may or may not be deal-prone. Stockpiling behavior might be exhibited by any buyer and can be very difficult to distinguish from increased consumption. For products that can be stored, putting a household in either a "new trier" category or a "very light user" category can be difficult. Finally, household behavior is subject to change over time. A switcher may become brand loyal. A brand loyal household may become dissatisfied with its brand and try several other brands before returning to the previous brand or converting to some other brand. Trade dealing or manufacturer couponing activity may trigger this process.

Background The frozen breakfast category provides a good example to study. Frozen breakfast products can be stockpiled in home freezers, although they are generally subject to some deterioration over time in the form of freezer burn. Hence, only limited stockpiling behavior is expected.

Frozen breakfast foods include frozen waffles, frozen pancake batter, frozen french toast, frozen pancakes, and some entree items, such as pancake and sausage combinations. The category is dominated by frozen waffles, which account for about 70 percent of the category volume. In a year, about 40 percent of all households purchase frozen waffles, with about 60 days between purchases. About 30 percent of category volume is sold with some form of trade deal. The trade deals are predominantly presented to consumers in the form of featured prices in advertising. About 10 percent of the volume is sold accompanied by the use of a manufacturer coupon. There are two primary flavors of frozen waffles, regular and buttermilk. A small amount of the sales volume is in specialty items, such as blueberry flavored.

The data used in this case study were collected from supermarket scanners that collect detailed purchasing history information from a sample or subset of households in the market. The market scanned in this case has a higher than average level of trade dealing. Table 5-1 provides a summary of a single year's purchasing by over 2,000 households, including non-buyers. Table 5-2 gives detailed purchase history on a number of selected individual households. Table 5-3 gives a breakdown of the volume of Eggo, one of the major brands in

Table 5-1
FROZEN WAFFLES PURCHASING

BRAND	PURCHASES	TOTAL	VOLUME IN POUNDS		
			W TRADE DEAL ONLY	W MFGR CPN ONLY	W MFGR CPN & TRADE DEAL
Market Total	7478	5942.22	2215.94	377.219	247.5
Aunt Jemima	2297	1735.97	345.00	264.781	167.8
Downyflake	616	630.75	284.38	11.063	8.2
Eggo	1701	1476.25	372.81	100.375	70.2
A/O Branded	6	4.50	0.00	0.000	0.0
PL/Generic	2858	2094.75	1213.75	1.000	1.2

Table 5-2
FROZEN WAFFLES PURCHASE HISTORIES - SELECTED PANELISTS

PANELNUM=51

WK	DAY	CHAIN	BRAND	SIZE	FLAVOR	UNIT	LBS. PURCH.	TOTAL $	PRICE / LB.	COUP VAL	MF CP	ST CP	ST FE
11	7	3	Downyflake	Small	B.Milk	1	0.75	0.77	1.03	.	.	.	.
13	7	3	Downyflake	Large	Regular	2	2.38	1.33	0.56	133	.	Y	.
35	6	3	Downyflake	Small	Other	1	0.75	0.78	1.04	.	.	.	Y
39	5	3	Downyflake	Small	Other	1	0.75	0.95	1.27	.	.	.	.

PANELNUM=1372

WK	DAY	CHAIN	BRAND	SIZE	FLAVOR	UNIT	LBS. PURCH.	TOTAL $	PRICE / LB.	COUP VAL	MF CP	ST CP	ST FE
1	4	4	Generic	XSmall	Regular	1	0.31	0.20	0.64	.	.	.	Y
8	4	4	Eggo	Small	Regular	1	0.69	0.88	1.28	.	.	.	.
10	4	4	A. Jemima	Small	Regular	7	4.38	3.74	0.85	20	Y	.	Y
18	4	4	A Jemima	Small	Regular	1	0.63	0.29	0.46	40	Y	.	Y
21	6	4	Eggo	Small	Regular	1	0.69	0.68	0.99	20	Y	.	.
23	6	3	A. Jemima	Small	Regular	1	0.63	0.89	1.42	.	.	.	.
24	4	4	A. Jemima	Large	Regular	2	1.88	1.76	0.94	.	.	.	Y
26	4	4	Eggo	Large	Regular	1	1.06	0.99	0.93	.	.	.	Y
30	4	4	Eggo	Small	Regular	2	1.38	1.18	0.86	.	.	.	Y
31	5	4	Generic	XSmall	Regular	1	0.31	0.20	0.64	.	.	.	Y
32	7	3	Eggo	Small	Regular	1	0.69	0.88	1.28	.	.	.	.
34	3	4	Eggo	Small	Regular	1	0.69	0.88	1.28	.	.	.	.
36	5	4	Eggo	Small	Regular	1	0.69	0.88	1.28	.	.	.	.
38	5	4	Eggo	Large	Regular	1	1.06	0.99	0.93	.	.	.	Y
38	6	4	Eggo	Large	Regular	1	1.06	0.99	0.93	.	.	.	Y
40	6	3	Downyflake	Small	Other	1	0.75	0.78	1.04	.	.	.	Y
42	4	4	A. Jemima	Small	Other	1	0.63	0.46	0.74	40	Y	.	.
44	4	4	A. Jemima	Small	Regular	2	1.25	0.72	0.58	30	Y	.	Y
50	6	3	Downyflake	Small	Regular	1	0.75	0.59	0.79	.	.	.	Y

Table 5-2 (CONTINUED)

PANELNUM=5639

WK	DAY	CHAIN	BRAND	SIZE	FLAVOR	UNIT	LBS. PURCH.	TOTAL $	PRICE /LB.	COUP VAL.	MF CP	ST CP	ST FE
5	5	3	A. Jemima	Large	Regular	1	0.94	1.29	1.38	.	.	.	.
7	6	3	A. Jemima	Large	Regular	1	0.94	1.18	1.26	.	.	.	.
8	6	3	Eggo	Large	Regular	1	1.06	1.49	1.40	.	.	.	.
9	5	3	Eggo	Large	Regular	1	1.06	1.49	1.40	.	.	.	.
11	5	3	Eggo	Large	Regular	1	1.06	1.25	1.18	.	.	.	.
12	5	3	Eggo	Large	Regular	1	1.06	1.25	1.18	.	.	.	.
13	5	3	Eggo	Large	Regular	1	1.06	1.25	1.18	.	.	.	.
14	5	3	Eggo	Large	Regular	1	1.06	1.49	1.40	.	.	.	.
21	5	3	A. Jemima	Large	Regular	1	0.94	1.29	1.38	.	.	.	.
22	6	3	A. Jemima	Large	Regular	1	0.94	1.29	1.38	.	.	.	.
23	5	3	A. Jemima	Small	B.Milk	1	0.63	0.89	1.42	.	.	.	.
27	5	3	Downyflake	Large	B.Milk	1	1.19	1.39	1.17	.	.	.	.
28	5	3	Downyflake	Large	B.Milk	1	1.19	1.39	1.17	.	.	.	.
30	5	3	Downyflake	Large	B.Milk	1	1.19	1.39	1.17	.	.	.	.
31	5	3	Eggo	Large	Regular	1	1.06	1.49	1.40	.	.	.	.
32	5	3	Eggo	Large	Regular	1	1.06	1.49	1.40	.	.	.	.
33	5	3	Downyflake	Large	B.Milk	1	1.19	1.39	1.17	.	.	.	.
35	5	3	A. Jemima	Large	Regular	1	0.94	1.29	1.38	.	.	.	.
37	5	3	Downyflake	Large	B.Milk	1	1.19	1.39	1.17	.	.	.	.
38	5	3	Downyflake	Large	Regular	1	1.19	1.23	1.04	.	.	.	.
40	6	3	A. Jemima	Small	B.Milk	1	0.63	0.56	0.90	30	Y	.	.

PANELNUM=7171

WK	DAY	CHAIN	BRAND	SIZE	FLAVOR	UNIT	LBS. PURCH.	TOTAL $	PRICE /LB.	COUP VAL	MF CP	ST CP	ST FE
1	4	4	PL/Generic	XSmall	Regular	2	0.63	0.40	0.64	.	.	.	Y
2	3	2	PL/Generic	XSmall	Regular	1	0.31	0.00	0.00	25	.	Y	Y
4	4	4	Eggo	Small	Regular	2	1.38	0.96	0.70	20	.	Y	Y
13	7	3	Downyflake	Large	Regular	2	2.38	1.33	0.56	133	.	Y	.
14	7	3	Downyflake	Large	Regular	2	2.38	1.33	0.56	133	.	Y	.
18	4	4	A. Jemima	Small	Regular	2	1.25	0.88	0.70	30	Y	.	Y
18	4	4	A. Jemima	Large	Regular	2	1.88	2.58	1.38	.	.	.	.
20	7	3	Downyflake	Small	Regular	2	1.50	0.95	0.63	95	.	Y	.
24	4	4	A. Jemima	Large	Regular	1	0.94	0.48	0.51	40	Y	.	Y
26	5	3	Downyflake	Small	B.Milk	1	0.75	0.78	1.04	.	.	.	Y
29	3	3	A. Jemima	Small	Other	1	0.63	0.36	0.58	40	Y	.	Y
29	3	3	A. Jemima	Small	B.Milk	1	0.63	0.46	0.74	30	Y	.	Y
30	5	3	PL/Generic	XSmall	Regular	1	0.31	0.20	0.64	.	.	.	.
30	6	3	A. Jemima	Small	Regular	1	0.63	0.56	0.90	20	Y	.	Y
32	4	3	PL/Generic	XSmall	Regular	2	0.63	0.40	0.64	.	.	.	Y
33	3	3	PL/Generic	XSmall	Regular	2	0.63	0.40	0.64	.	.	.	Y
34	7	2	Downyflake	Small	Regular	1	0.75	0.49	0.65	20	Y	.	Y
36	6	3	PL/Generic	XSmall	Regular	2	0.63	0.40	0.64	.	.	.	.
37	5	3	PL/Generic	XSmall	Regular	2	0.63	0.40	0.64	.	.	.	.
38	3	4	Eggo	Large	Regular	1	1.06	0.99	0.93	.	.	.	Y
39	3	3	PL/Generic	XSmall	Regular	2	0.63	0.40	0.64	.	.	.	Y
39	5	2	PL/Generic	Small	Regular	1	0.69	0.59	0.86	.	.	.	Y

Table 5-2 (CONTINUED)

WK	DAY	CHAIN	BRAND	SIZE	FLAVOR	UNIT	LBS. PURCH.	TOTAL $	PRICE / LB.	COUP VAL	MF CP	ST CP	ST FE
40	1	3	Downyflake	Small	B.Milk	1	0.75	0.78	1.04	.	.	.	Y
40	5	4	PL/Generic	XSmall	Regular	3	0.94	0.60	0.64	.	.	.	.
40	7	4	PL/Generic	XSmall	Regular	3	0.94	0.60	0.64	.	.	.	.
41	1	3	A. Jemima	Small	Regular	2	1.25	1.36	1.09	.	.	.	Y
45	5	3	A. Jemima	Small	Regular	1	0.63	0.68	1.09	.	.	.	.
48	6	3	PL/Generic	XSmall	Regular	2	0.63	0.40	0.64	.	.	.	Y
49	7	3	Downyflake	Small	B.Milk	1	0.75	0.59	0.79	.	.	.	Y
49	7	3	Downyflake	Small	Regular	1	0.75	0.59	0.79	.	.	.	.
51	2	3	Downyflake	Small	B.Milk	1	0.75	0.59	0.79	.	.	.	Y
51	2	3	Downyflake	Small	Regular	1	0.75	0.59	0.79	.	.	.	Y
52	3	3	Downyflake	Small	B.Milk	1	0.75	0.59	0.79	.	.	.	Y

PANELNUM=10886

WK	DAY	CHAIN	BRAND	SIZE	FLAVOR	UNIT	LBS. PURCH.	TOTAL $	PRICE / LB.	COUP VAL	MF CP	ST CP	ST FE
13	5	3	Eggo	Large	Regular	1	1.06	1.05	0.99	20	Y	.	.
14	5	3	Downyflake	Large	Regular	2	2.38	1.33	0.56	133	.	Y	.
18	6	3	Downyflake	Large	Regular	1	1.19	1.23	1.04	.	.	.	.
19	6	3	Downyflake	Large	Regular	3	3.56	2.97	0.83	.	.	.	Y
20	5	3	Downyflake	Small	Regular	2	1.50	0.95	0.63	95	.	Y	.
28	5	3	Downyflake	Large	Regular	1	1.19	0.94	0.79	.	.	.	.
29	5	3	Eggo	Large	Regular	2	2.13	2.98	1.40	.	.	.	.
30	5	3	Eggo	Large	Regular	2	2.13	2.98	1.40	.	.	.	.
31	5	3	Eggo	Large	Regular	2	2.13	2.98	1.40	.	.	.	.
32	5	3	Eggo	Large	Regular	1	1.06	1.49	1.40	.	.	.	.
42	5	3	Eggo	Large	Regular	2	2.13	2.98	1.40	.	.	.	.
46	4	3	Eggo	Large	Regular	2	2.13	2.98	1.40	.	.	.	.

PANELNUM=11827

WK	DAY	CHAIN	BRAND	SIZE	FLAVOR	UNIT	LBS. PURCH.	TOTAL $	PRICE / LB.	COUP VAL	MF CP	ST CP	ST FE
4	2	4	Eggo	Small	Regular	1	0.69	0.68	0.99	.	.	.	Y
14	7	4	Eggo	Small	Regular	1	0.69	0.69	1.00	.	.	.	Y
24	7	4	A. Jemima	Large	Regular	2	1.88	1.76	0.94	.	.	.	Y
26	7	4	Eggo	Large	Regular	2	2.13	1.98	0.93	.	.	.	Y
30	1	4	Eggo	Small	Regular	4	2.75	2.36	0.86	.	.	.	Y
35	7	4	A. Jemima	Small	Regular	4	2.50	2.72	1.09	.	.	.	Y
38	7	4	Eggo	Large	Regular	2	2.13	1.98	0.93	.	.	.	Y
44	7	4	A. Jemima	Small	Regular	2	1.25	1.02	0.82	30	Y	.	Y

PANELNUM=15935

WK	DAY	CHAIN	BRAND	SIZE	FLAVOR	UNIT	LBS. PURCH.	TOTAL $	PRICE / LB.	COUP VAL	MF CP	ST CP	ST FE
1	5	3	PL/Generic	XSmall	Regular	2	0.63	0.40	0.64	.	.	.	.
14	5	3	Downyflake	Large	Regular	2	2.38	1.33	0.56	133	.	Y	.

Table 5-2 (CONTINUED)

47	4	3	PL/Generic	XSmall	Regular	2	0.63	0.66	1.06	.	.	.	.
50	3	3	Downyflake	Small	Other	1	0.75	0.59	0.79	.	.	.	Y
50	3	3	Downyflake	Small	Regular	1	0.75	0.59	0.79	.	.	.	Y
52	2	3	Downyflake	Small	B.Milk	2	1.50	1.18	0.79	.	.	.	Y

PANELNUM=18970

WK	DAY	CHAIN	BRAND	SIZE	FLAVOR	UNIT	LBS. PURCH.	TOTAL $	PRICE / LB.	COUP VAL	MF CP	ST CP	ST FE
6	6	2	Downyflake	Small	Regular	1	0.75	0.89	1.19	.	.	.	.
12	6	2	Downyflake	Small	Regular	1	0.75	0.89	1.19	.	.	.	.
16	4	2	Downyflake	Large	Regular	1	1.19	1.33	1.12	.	.	.	.
17	6	2	Downyflake	Small	Regular	1	0.75	0.89	1.19	.	.	.	.
20	6	2	Downyflake	Small	Regular	1	0.75	0.89	1.19	.	.	.	.
21	6	2	Downyflake	Small	Regular	1	0.75	0.89	1.19	.	.	.	.
22	6	2	Downyflake	Small	Regular	1	0.75	0.89	1.19	.	.	.	.
23	6	2	Downyflake	Large	Regular	1	1.19	1.29	1.09	.	.	.	.
27	6	2	Downyflake	Large	Regular	1	1.19	1.33	1.12	.	.	.	.
31	6	2	Downyflake	Small	Regular	1	0.75	0.79	1.05	.	.	.	Y
32	6	2	Downyflake	Large	Regular	1	1.19	1.33	1.12	.	.	.	.
33	6	2	Downyflake	Large	Regular	1	1.19	1.33	1.12	.	.	.	.
34	6	2	Downyflake	Large	Regular	1	1.19	1.33	1.12	.	.	.	.
37	6	2	Downyflake	Large	Regular	1	1.19	1.33	1.12	.	.	.	.
39	7	2	Downyflake	Large	Regular	1	1.19	1.33	1.12	.	.	.	.
43	6	2	Downyflake	Small	Regular	1	0.75	0.89	1.19	.	.	.	.
45	6	2	Downyflake	Small	Regular	1	0.75	0.79	1.05	.	.	.	.
46	5	2	Downyflake	Small	Regular	1	0.75	0.89	1.19	.	.	.	.
47	6	2	Downyflake	Large	Regular	1	1.19	1.29	1.09	.	.	.	Y
51	7	2	Downyflake	Small	B.Milk	1	0.75	0.89	1.19	.	.	.	.
52	6	2	Downyflake	Small	B.Milk	1	0.75	0.99	1.32	.	.	.	.

PANELNUM=79741

WK	DAY	CHAIN	BRAND	SIZE	FLAVOR	UNIT	LBS. PURCH.	TOTAL $	PRICE / LB.	COUP VAL	MF CP	ST CP	ST FE
1	6	4	Eggo	Large	Regular	1	1.06	1.49	1.40	.	.	.	.
3	5	4	Eggo	Large	Regular	1	1.06	1.49	1.40	.	.	.	.
3	7	3	Downyflake	Large	Regular	1	1.19	1.33	1.12	.	.	.	.
9	7	2	Eggo	Large	Regular	2	2.13	2.78	1.31	.	.	.	.
9	7	2	Eggo	Small	Other	1	0.69	0.99	1.44	.	.	.	.
19	1	4	A. Jemima	Large	Regular	1	0.94	1.29	1.38	.	.	.	.
19	1	4	A. Jemima	Small	Other	1	0.63	0.89	1.42	.	.	.	.
20	5	4	Eggo	Large	Regular	1	1.06	1.49	1.40	.	.	.	.
20	5	4	A. Jemima	Small	Other	1	0.63	0.89	1.42	.	.	.	.
21	3	4	A. Jemima	Small	Other	2	1.25	1.78	1.42	.	.	.	.
21	5	2	Eggo	Large	Regular	2	2.13	2.78	1.31	.	.	.	.
21	5	2	Downyflake	Small	Other	1	0.75	0.95	1.27	.	.	.	.
24	5	4	A. Jemima	Small	B.Milk	1	0.63	0.89	1.42	.	.	.	.
24	5	4	A. Jemima	Small	Other	1	0.63	0.89	1.42	.	.	.	.
24	7	2	Eggo	Large	Regular	1	1.06	1.39	1.31	.	.	.	.

Table 5-2 (CONTINUED)

25	6	2	Eggo	Large	Regular	2	2.13	2.38	1.12	.	.	.	Y
26	1	2	Eggo	Large	Regular	1	1.06	1.39	1.31	.	.	.	.
29	6	4	Eggo	Large	Regular	2	2.13	2.98	1.40	.	.	.	.
35	7	2	Eggo	Large	Regular	1	1.06	1.19	1.12	.	.	.	Y
40	7	2	Eggo	Large	Regular	1	1.06	1.29	1.21	.	.	.	Y
43	1	2	Eggo	Large	Regular	1	1.06	1.39	1.31	.	.	.	.
48	6	2	A. Jemima	Small	Other	1	0.63	0.89	1.42	.	.	.	.

PANELNUM=83858

WK	DAY	CHAIN	BRAND	SIZE	FLAVOR	UNIT	LBS. PURCH.	TOTAL $	PRICE /LB.	COUP VAL	MF CP	ST CP	ST FE
1	2	3	Downyflake	Large	Regular	1	1.19	1.33	1.12	.	.	.	.
3	2	3	Downyflake	Large	Regular	1	1.19	1.33	1.12	.	.	.	.
10	3	3	Downyflake	Large	Regular	1	1.19	1.3	1.12	.	.	.	.
13	2	3	Downyflake	Large	Regular	1	1.19	1.33	1.12	.	.	.	.
14	2	3	Downyflake	Large	Regular	2	2.38	1.33	0.56	133	.	Y	.
26	2	3	Downyflake	Small	Regular	1	075	0.78	1.04	.	.	.	Y
31	2	3	Downyflake	Large	Regular	1	1.19	1.23	1.04	.	.	.	.
34	2	3	Downyflake	Large	Regular	1	1.19	1.03	0.87	20	Y	.	.
37	2	3	Downyflake	Large	Regular	1	1.19	1.23	1.04	.	.	.	.
40	3	3	Downyflake	Large	Regular	1	1.19	1.23	1.04	.	.	.	.
43	3	3	Downyflake	Large	Regular	1	1.19	1.23	1.04	.	.	.	.
50	2	3	Downyflake	Large	Regular	1	1.19	1.23	1.04	.	.	.	.
52	3	3	Downyflake	Large	Regular	1	1.19	1.23	1.04	.	.	.	.

PANELNUM=87934

WK	DAY	CHAIN	BRAND	SIZE	FLAVOR	UNIT	LBS. PURCH.	TOTAL $	PRICE /LB.	COUP VAL	MF CP	ST CP	ST FE
2	2	2	PL/Generic	XSmall	Regular	1	0.31	0.00	0.00	25	.	Y	Y
10	3	2	PL/Generic	XSmall	Regular	1	0.31	0.25	0.80	.	.	.	.
13	2	2	Eggo	Large	Regular	1	1.06	1.19	1.12	.	.	.	Y
14	2	2	Eggo	Large	Regular	1	1.06	1.19	1.12	.	.	.	.
25	2	2	Eggo	Small	Regular	1	0.69	0.88	1.28	.	.	.	.
35	2	2	Eggo	Large	Regular	1	1.06	1.19	1.12	.	.	.	Y
38	3	4	Eggo	Large	Regular	1	1.06	0.99	0.93	.	.	.	Y
50	3	4	Eggo	Large	Regular	1	1.06	0.96	0.90	.	.	.	Y

PANELNUM=91373

WK	DAY	CHAIN	BRAND	SIZE	FLAVOR	UNIT	LBS. PURCH.	TOTAL $	PRICE /LB.	COUP VAL	MF CP	ST CP	ST FE
2	5	2	PL/Generic	XSmall	Regular	1	0.31	0.00	0.00	25	.	Y	Y
2	5	2	Eggo	Small	Regular	1	0.69	0.88	1.28	.	.	.	.
3	7	2	Eggo	Small	Regular	1	0.69	0.88	1.28	.	.	.	.
10	5	2	Eggo	Small	Regular	1	0.69	0.88	1.28	.	.	.	.
14	5	2	Eggo	Large	Regular	1	1.06	1.19	1.12	.	.	.	.
17	7	2	Eggo	Small	B.Milk	1	0.69	0.89	1.29	.	.	.	.

Table 5-2 (CONTINUED)

19	5	2	Eggo	Small	Regular	1	0.69	0.88	1.28	.	.	.	.
24	7	2	Eggo	Small	B.Milk	1	0.69	0.89	1.29	.	.	.	.
27	7	2	Eggo	Small	B.Milk	1	0.69	0.59	0.86	30	Y	.	.
32	7	2	Eggo	Small	B.Milk	1	0.69	0.89	1.29	.	.	.	Y
35	7	2	Eggo	Large	Regular	1	1.06	1.19	1.12	.	.	.	Y
37	6	2	Eggo	Small	B.Milk	1	0.69	0.89	1.29	.	.	.	.
39	7	2	Eggo	Small	B.Milk	1	0.69	0.89	1.29	.	.	.	.
40	7	2	Eggo	Large	Regular	1	1.06	1.29	1.21	.	.	.	Y
41	7	2	Eggo	Small	B.Milk	1	0.69	0.89	1.29	.	.	.	.
43	7	2	Eggo	Small	B.Milk	1	0.69	0.89	1.29	.	.	.	.
44	7	2	Eggo	Small	B.Milk	1	0.69	0.89	1.29	.	.	.	.
46	5	2	A. Jemima	Small	Other	1	0.63	0.39	0.62	40	Y	.	Y
47	5	2	Eggo	Small	B.Milk	1	0.69	0.89	1.29	.	.	.	.
52	6	2	Eggo	Small	B.Milk	1	0.69	0.89	1.29	.	.	.	.

Table 5-3
EGGO FROZEN WAFFLES VOLUME SOURCES BY BUYER GROUPING

BUYER GROUP	PURCHASE COUNTS	VOLUME SALES IN POUNDS			
		TOTAL	WITH TRADE DEAL ONLY	WITH MFG. COUPON ONLY	WITH TRADE & MFR. COUPON
Total Eggo Purchase Activity	1701	1476.3	372.8	100.4	70.2
Eggo Loyal - Hi Deal	71	67.3	23.8	8.3	4.6
Eggo Loyal - Lo Deal	679	563.1	80.2	28.7	10.3
Other Loyal - Hi Deal	30	25.4	10.2	4.1	4.2
Other Loyal - Lo Deal	36	30.1	6.3	2.1	3.1
Non Loyal - Hi Deal	421	382.2	184.7	35.7	39.6
Non Loyal - Lo Deal	426	371.5	49.5	20.1	6.0
Light Buyers	0	0.0	0.0	0.0	0.0
One-Time buyers	38	36.6	18.2	1.4	2.4

the frozen waffle category, based upon a purchasing behavior classification scheme.

Question 1   Aunt Jemima and Eggo purchasers accounted for most of the redemption of manufacturer coupons. Using Table 5-1, what interactions do you find between purchasing with manufacturer coupons, and purchasing with trade deals for these brands?

Question 2   Some of the trade deal volume is incremental to the category, the rest is reshuffling among the brands. Using Table 5-1, estimate what the impact on Downyflake and its competitors would have been if only Downyflake trade dealing had been eliminated for each of the following assumptions:
a. All trade deal volume for Downyflake is incremental to both the brand and the category.
b. None of the trade deal volume is incremental to the category, and the Downyflake trade deal volume would be redistributed across all brands in the category, including Downyflake, in proportion to their total sales.

c. None of the trade deal volume is incremental to the category, and the Downyflake trade deal volume would be redistributed across all brands in the category, except Downyflake, in proportion to their sales on trade deal.

Question 3   Repeat Question 2 for Eggo instead of Downyflake.

Question 4   Contrast the results obtained from Questions 2 and 3.

Question 5   Review the individual panelist purchasing histories given in Table 5-2. Comment on the differing types of purchase behavior shown, the apparent importance of trade dealing and manufacturer coupons in the purchase decisions, and the stability of purchase behavior over time.

Question 6   Using Table 5-3 as the basis, discuss the importance of each buyer group to:
• Eggo sales without trade deal or manufacturer coupon
• Eggo sales with trade deal
• Eggo sales with manufacturer coupon
• Eggo total sales

Question 7   Discuss the probable impact on Eggo sales in this market of:
• Eliminating manufacturer coupon drops
• A 10% reduction in trade dealing activity

Question 8 (Optional)   The method of constructing the buyer groups defined in Table 5-3 carries the potential for generating biased results. Since brand loyalty was defined as 75 percent or more of total volume in a single brand, these households are severely restricted in the amount of volume they can contribute to other brands. In categories with very frequent purchases, an alternative is to classify households during some base period, and then analyze their purchasing behavior in a subsequent time period. Discuss other potential sources of bias with either analysis procedure.

Households were classified on total purchasing behavior by the following method:
   One-time buyers—purchased frozen waffles only once.
   Light buyers—purchased frozen waffles two or three times.

Households purchasing four or more times were classified on two dimensions:
   Deal sensitivity—Low deal sensitivity if their volume purchased with trade deal and manufacturer coupon was less than market average. High deal sensitivity if their volume purchased with trade deal and manufacturer coupon was market average or more.
   Brand loyalty—Brand loyal if at least 75 percent of their purchase volume was in one specific brand, and non-loyal if no one brand accounted for at least 75 percent of total purchase volume. Households loyal to brands other than Eggo were combined into the "loyal to other brands" group.

6 *Principles of Sales Promotion*

Based upon the discussion and cases provided, there are ten principles of sales promotion that can be summarized. These ten principles should serve well as managerial guidelines for those responsible for the administration of sales promotion programs.

Store Level Data Is Critically Important

Aggregate market level data simply are not sufficiently sensitive to detect the true sales impacts of promotional programs. Data must be measured at the individual store level and analyzed on at least a weekly basis to understand the dynamics of sales promotion. Even when the analysis is for a single chain in a single market, analysis should be at the individual store level. Promotions, particularly in-store display or shelf price reduction, may not be equally effective across stores, thus affecting profit optimization. Results from individual level analyses can be combined into a chain or market summary.

Sales Volume Is the Key Measure

While market share as a measure of sales performance has a strong tradition, competitive activity and other factors make it insufficiently sensitive to measure the short-term impact of sales promotion. The promoted brand's sales volume is by far the best measure of the performance of a sales promotion program.

Trade Promotions Should Generate Incremental Profit

One of the most important findings from the analysis of scanner-based data is the consistent return to the base level of business for a brand after a promotional period. In other words, there does not seem to be any future sales increase that results from the promotion. The promotion generally stimulates sales only during the promotional period. This clearly means that the promotion itself should generate incremental profit to be justified.

Package Size Is Important

Not all consumers favor the same package size, despite their interest in the product. It is critically important to promote the package size that matches the appropriate market for the promotion to be a success.

The Demand Curve Is Kinked

For the first time, marketing managers can begin with a realistic empirically estimated demand curve. Both pricing and promotion decisions can be made on the basis of the fundamental understanding of the relationship of price and sales volume for the product category and brand. In many product categories, that demand curve is clearly kinked, meaning that lowering the price in certain ranges will not necessarily result in increasing the sales volume, or that raising the price will not necessarily result in greatly decreased sales volume. Obviously, knowledge of the existence of the kinks, if they exist, greatly improves the possibility of estimating the increased revenue potential for the brand.

Direct Competitive Effects Are Minimal Except Among Switchers

Despite common sense expectation, promoting one brand in a product category has very little impact on loyal purchasers of other brands. In other words, a sales promotion program does not necessarily cut into the competing brand's business. Promotion clearly has the greatest impact on brand switchers. It is the switchers that promotion is most likely to influence, with additional volume potential available from infrequent category buyers. Promotion may stimulate overall category consumption.

Price Sensitivity and Promotion Responsiveness Are Different

Not all brands respond in the same way to price, depending upon the loyalty characteristics of the brand. Some products may well behave entirely on the basis of price, as if they were nothing but a commodity. Impulse-driven items may respond primarily to promotion elements such as in-store display.

Retail Trade Performance Is Essential

Even the most successful consumer promotions can be substantially enhanced by the trade. The cooperation of the trade with in-store displays, ad features, and their own promotional programs creates a special synergy that generally results in sales that far exceed what either the manufacturer or retailer could do alone.

Reduction of Promotion Results in Loss of Volume

Generally every time a promotion program ends, the sales volume substantially declines. Clearly there is a strong relationship between the promotion and the sales volume for the brand. However, the loss of sales volume does not necessarily mean that profit is lost. The lost revenue due to lower prices and the cost of the promotion itself may mean lower profit during the promotion.

Profit Can Be Maximized through Analysis of Real Data

The most important point of this discussion is that promotional programs should be analyzed in terms of the incremental sales generated and the additional costs incurred. Local competitive conditions and volume response differences can lead to dramatically different profitability from region to region for apparently similar promotional activity. The profitability of the promotional program should be the ultimate criterion for the management of promotional programs after the initial brand introduction.

References

Box, G. E. P., and G. M. Jenkins, *Time Series Analysis: Forecasting and Control*, revised edition, San Francisco: Holden-Day, 1976.

Fuller, Wayne A., *Introduction to Statistical Time Series*, New York: John Wiley & Sons, 1976.

Nelson, C. R., *Applied Time Series for Managerial Forecasting*, San Francisco: Holden-Day, 1973.

Montgomery, D. C., and L. A. Johnson, *Forecasting and Time Series Analysis*, New York: McGraw-Hill, 1976.

Pindyck, R. S., and D. L. Rubinfeld, *Econometric Models and Economic Forecasts*, part 3, New York: McGraw-Hill, 1976.

Index

Index